A. (Alexandre) Sauzay

Wonders of Glass-making in all Ages

A. (Alexandre) Sauzay

Wonders of Glass-making in all Ages

ISBN/EAN: 9783743309807

Manufactured in Europe, USA, Canada, Australia, Japa

Cover: Foto ©ninafisch / pixelio.de

Manufactured and distributed by brebook publishing software (www.brebook.com)

A. (Alexandre) Sauzay

Wonders of Glass-making in all Ages

WONDERS OF ART AND ARCHÆOLOGY

WONDERS

OF

GLASS-MAKING

IN ALL AGES

BY

A. SAUZAY

ILLUSTRATED

NEW YORK
CHARLES SCRIBNER'S SONS
1885

ALPHABETICAL TABLE OF CONTENTS.

	PAGE.
ACHROMATISM.—Its etymology—What it is—How obtained—Its inventors..	264
ANNEALING	71
ARISTOTLE.—Mentions plated glass being used as mirrors..........	93
BACCARAT.—Offshoot from a Belgian glass factory...............	56
BACON (FRANCIS).—Quoted.......................................	194
—— (ROGER).—Supposed inventor of telescopes...............	303
BARTHÉLÉMY (L'ABBÉ).—Quoted.................................	219
BEADS FOR NECKLACES AND CHAPLETS:—	
—— Their antiquity..	25
—— Manufacture...	205
BELGIUM.—Glass-works...	56
BEROVIERO (ANGELO).—Venetian glass-maker—His history.......	46
BERRY (DUCHESSE DE).—Had squares of oiled linen in her windows (1413)..	80
BINOCULAR GLASSES.—See Opera Glasses.	
BOHEMIA.—Possessed glass-works of its own at an early period...	49
—— Its method of manufacture................................	51
—— Style of ornament.......................................	50, 147
—— Glass in the Cluny Museum...............................	50
—— Cause of the cheapness of its production.................	51
—— Wages of the workmen....................................	52
BONTEMPS (M.)—Quoted on the manufacture of filigree glass.....	224
—— On the composition of flint glass........................	265
—— And of crown glass.......................................	268

TABLE OF CONTENTS.

	PAGE
BONZI (FRANÇOIS DE).—Reply to Colbert	117
BORDA improves lighthouses	312
BOTTLES.—History	126
—— Their manufacture	129
—— Made in a mould	130
—— Venetian	131
BOUDET (M.).—Quoted	207
BOUTET DE MONVEL.—Quoted; his definition of optical instruments	257
BREWSTER (SIR DAVID) mentions a crystal lens found amongst the ruins of Nineveh	259
CAMERA LUCIDA.—Its results	287
CARILLON (M.).—Inventor of the mould for bottles	130
CHAMPAGNE.—Was this wine known in the 16th century?	154
CHAN.—Chinese emperor and astronomer	259
CHANCE (MESSRS.).—Quoted on English glass	56
CHEVALIER (ARTHUR).—Quoted on the manufacture of optical glass	271
CLAUDET.—Analysis of Pompeian window glass	78
CLICHY-LA-GARENNE.—Three glasses from these crystal works	154
—— A glass jug	135
—— Engraved crystals	166
CLOCK GLASSES	235
COCHIN (M. A.).—Quoted on the composition of glass	68
—— On glass-founding	120
COLBERT.—Founds the first glass-works at Paris	116
CONTANT D'ORVILLE.—Quoted	156
COLORING OF GLASS AND CRYSTAL.—What Strabo says of it	207
—— Mentioned by Herodotus	209
—— How well the ancients imitated precious stones	209
—— Anecdote of the Emperor Gallienus	210
—— Its manufacture for a long time abandoned in France	212
—— On the processes employed in making artificial precious stones	214
—— Method of cutting them	216
COUNCIL OF TEN.—Its tyrannical laws	45

TABLE OF CONTENTS.

	PAGE.
CROWN GLASS.—Used in optics	268
—— Manufacture	269
DARU.—Quoted	44
DEBETTE.—Quoted on the manufacture of crown glass	268
DESMARETS (REGNIER).—Quoted	114
DÉVÉRIA (M. TH.).—Translation of hieroglyphic inscription	25
DOLLOND discovers achromatism	263
—— improves compound microscope	279
DONNÉ AND FOUCAULT (MESSRS.) invent photo-electric microscope	292
DREBBEL (CORNELIUS VAN).—Mentioned	194, 278
DROLENVAUX (HUGH).—Erroneously supposed to have been the first to introduce glass-blowing into France	81
DUMAS (M.) on the composition of strass	214
DUPRÉ (ATHANASE).—Quoted on the marvels of the microscope	285
ENGLAND.—Glass manufactures	57
ENGRAVING ON GLASS AND CRYSTAL.—Its antiquity	27, 163
—— When introduced into Bohemia	165
—— Moderns not inferior in this art	169
—— Method of engraving glass and crystal	165
—— Imitation of engraved glass	170
EULER.—Recomposes light which had been decomposed by Newton	264
EYES, ARTIFICIAL.—Known to the Egyptians under several names	318
—— Successive improvements	321
—— How they are now made	323
FIESQUE (COMTESSE DE).—What she gave for a mirror	119
FIGUIER (LOUIS).—Quoted	283, 301
FLINT GLASS.—Used in optics—Manufacture	265
FLUDD (ROBERT).—Mentioned	194
FLÛTE.—Old-fashioned French drinking-glass	158
FORTUNATUS.—His letter to Queen Radegonde	60
FRANCE.—Antiquity of its glass-works	59
—— Gallo-Roman glass-works	59
—— Glass dishes used in the reign of Clotaire I	60
—— The price at which the privilege of glass-workers was granted by Humbert de Viennois	60

TABLE OF CONTENTS.

	PAGE
FRESNEL (AUGUSTIN) improves lighthouses	314
FRITTING	72
FURNACES	73
FUSCH.—Inventor of soluble glass	238
GALILEO (GALILEI) invents the opera glass	306
GALLIENUS.—Anecdote of this emperor	210
GAUBIL (PÈRE).—Quoted	259
GENTLEMEN GLASS-MAKERS.—What we are to understand by this	62
—— Lines from the poet Maynard	63
—— Opinion of B. Palissy	63
GERMANY.—Overthrows the Venetian monopoly	49
—— Style of ornament	50, 142
—— Names of the best workmen	49
—— Most ancient German vase	49
GILDING ON GLASS	159
—— Venetian glass sprinkled with gold	161
—— Mode of manufacture	161
—— Mode of manufacture in Bohemia	52
GLASS.—Its composition according to M. Cochin	68
—— Was it discovered accidentally by the Phœnicians?	23
—— Known to the Thebans	24
—— Most ancient object known in glass	25
—— The Romans imposed it as a tribute on the Egyptians	27
—— Theatre of Scaurus	28
—— Objects in use at Rome	32
—— Its manufacture introduced into Gaul	36
—— Strasbourg vase a proof of this	37
—— Art of glass-making lost in the West	38
—— Venice obtains the monopoly	43
—— Tyranny of the Council of Ten	45
—— History of Angelo Beroviero	46
—— Venice begins to export glass	47
—— Germany throws off the yoke of Venetian monopoly	49
—— Bohemia follows its example	49
—— Belgian glass-making	56

TABLE OF CONTENTS.

	PAGE
GLASS.—Numerous glass-works in England.............	57
—— French glass-works.........................	59
—— Dishes used in the time of Clotaire I.............	59
—— Service for Mad. Diane......................	61
—— Cause of iridescence in glass..................	180
—— Glasses for watches and clocks................	234
—— Reason that glass breaks so often..............	71
GLASS COMPOSED OF TWO LAYERS:—	
—— Manufacture..............................	173
—— How to procure the layers of different colors......	173
—— Portland vase.............................	173
—— FILIGREE.—What is meant by..................	219
—— —— Known to the Romans..................	219
—— —— Manufacture.........................	220
—— —— How vases are made...................	228
—— FROSTED.—Two methods of making it	182
—— GROUND.................................	236
—— LACE.—Mode of obtaining the design...........	172
—— SOLUBLE.—By whom invented.................	238
—— SPUN.—Manufacture........................	189
—— —— To what degree of fineness it may be brought..	191
—— —— The lion with glass hair................	191
—— —— Fabrics for dresses made with it..........	190
GOBLETS AND DRINKING GLASSES....................	139
—— What kind was preferred at Rome..............	140
—— German; meaning of wiederkommen............	145
—— Venetian; on their shapes...................	147
—— French, of the time of Henri II...............	156
—— Champagne; was champagne drunk in the 16th century?..	156
—— from the crystal works of Clichy-la-Garenne......	154
—— called *Flûtes*............................	158
GREGORY.—Telescope............................	299
GUGNON.—Process for the decoration of lace glass......	172
HALL.—Inventor of achromatism...................	263
HENRI III.—Mirror..............................	111
HERODOTUS.—Quoted on colored glass...............	209

TABLE OF CONTENTS.

	PAGE
HERSCHEL (SIR WILLIAM).—Telescope	301
HOEFER.—Quoted	195
HORACE.—Quoted	127
HUMPHRY (TEMPLE).—Inventor of a fresh system for lighthouses	316
IRIDESCENCE OF GLASS.—To what is it to be attributed?	180
JET.—Not a new fashion	201
—— First used in Egypt	203
JUG from the crystal works of Clichy	135
LABARTE (M. J.)—Quoted 45, 50, 166,	228
LACTANTIUS	79
LADLE	72
LAMBOURG.—Makes a lion with hairs of spun glass	191
LANÇON.—Quoted on the cutting of artificial precious stones	216
LANTERN, MAGIC.—The origin of microscopes	290
LATTICINIO.—What the Italians mean by this word	219
LAZARI.—Quoted	94
LIBRI.—Quoted	194
LIEBERKUHN.—Inventor of the solar microscope	290
LIGHT.—What it was a century ago	260
—— When decomposed shows seven colors	264
—— How recomposed	264
LIGHTHOUSES.—Antiquity	309
—— Successive improvements	310
—— Difference between them	310
—— With a continuous whistle	316
LIPPERSHEY (JOHN).—Optician of Middelbourg	304
LOOKING-GLASSES.—See Mirrors.	
MACY.—Makes bottles in the reign of Philip the Fair	128
MARIE DE MEDICI.—Description of her mirror	98
MARION (F.).—Quoted	279
MARTIAL.—What he says on bottles	128
MARVER	72

	PAGE
MAYNARD.—Verses against the poet St. Amand	62
METIUS (JAMES).—Supposed inventor of the telescope	303
MICROMETER.—Of what use	283
MICROSCOPE, SIMPLE	277
—— COMPOUND	278
—— Two learned men claim the merit of the discovery	278
—— Services it renders	281
—— Wonderful effects	284
—— Its effects retained by the Nachet prism	286
—— Solar—By whom invented	290
—— Photo-electric—Inventors	292
MILLEFIORI	231
MILLENGEN.—Quoted	173
MILTON.—Description of the first mirror	89
MIRRORS.—History	89
—— Earliest of which there is any record	91
—— METALLIC, of the Egyptians	91
—— —— Egg-shaped	91
—— Of obsidian	92
—— Whether the ancients understood plating	93
—— Aristotle mentions it	93
—— Sidon celebrated for its glass mirrors	93
—— First manufactory of silvered glasses in Flanders	95
—— The Venetians made silvered glasses in the 14th century	94
—— The Venetians seized the monopoly	95
—— The privilege granted to Andrea and Domenico d'Anzolo	95
—— Cause of the small size of the oldest mirrors	96
—— That belonging to Marie de Medici	98
—— Its valuation in 1791	101
—— Italian metallic mirror with carved wood frame	105
—— Round, with valves in carved ivory	107
—— Round hand, bearing a device	108
—— of Henri III	111
—— Infatuation of the public for Italian work	112
—— Colbert commands workmen to be sent from Murano	115
—— Reply of François de Bonzi	116
—— Colbert founds glass-works at Paris with Venetian workmen	116

TABLE OF CONTENTS.

	PAGE
MIRRORS.—Continued under Lucas de Nehou	117
—— History of some young Strasbourgeois	117
—— Price given for a mirror by the Comtesse de Fiesque	119
—— Account of the founding of a looking-glass at St. Gobain	121
—— New method of silvering invented by M. Petitjean	124
MONTAIGNE.—Quoted	145
NACHET (MM.).—Invent a prism	286
NEHOU (LUCAS DE) placed at the head of the royal glass-works	117
—— (LOUIS LUCAS DE) invented the founding of glass	120
NEWTON (SIR ISAAC) the first to decompose light	261
—— His telescope	299
NIEUPOORT.—Quoted on Roman funerals	32
NORTHUMBERLAND (DUKE OF).—Glass taken out of his windows when he moved	80
OPERA GLASSES	309
OPTICAL GLASSES	257
—— Whether the ancients possessed them	258
—— Shapes of the lenses	270
PALISSY (BERNARD).—His opinion of gentlemen glass-makers	68
PEARLS, FALSE.—Antiquity	241
—— What Petronius says of them	241
—— A corporation formed at Venice under the name of pearl and paternoster makers	245
—— Story of Jacquin	251
—— Mode of coloring pearls	256
PÉLIGOT 69, 71, 75, 78, 83, 84, 87, 121, 170, 180, 214, 239,	266
PETRONIUS.—Quoted 127,	241
PILON (EMILE).—Artificial eyes	322
PLINY.—Quoted 22, 27, 92, 209,	242
PLUTARCH.—Quoted	91
PONTY	72
PORTA (J. B.).—Supposed inventor of telescopes	303
PORTLAND VASE	175
POTS	75
PRISM.—Its form and effects	262

TABLE OF CONTENTS.

	PAGE
RADEGONDE.—Letter of Fortunatus to that queen	60
RAKE	72
RA-MA-KA.—Bead from her necklace	26
RÉAUMUR on spun glass	192
REIMMAN.—His opinion on the invention of glass	22
ROBINET.—Invents a pump	87
ROUSSIN (DR.).—Quoted	283
SAINT GOBAIN.—Its foundation	120
—— Description of glass-founding as practised there	121
SAINT SIMON.—Quoted	119
SALVINO D'ARMATO.—Invents spectacles	275
SANCTORIUS.—Mentioned	195
SAVARY.—Quoted on jet	202
SCAURUS.—Theatre	28
SENECA.—Speaks of globes filled with water used as magnifying glasses	259
SHEARS	73
SKIMMING	73
SOLAR SPECTRUM	262
SPECTACLES.—History	274
—— Inventor	275
STONES, IMITATION.—See coloring of glass.	
STRABO.—On the coloring of glass	207
STRASBOURG.—Young men from this town discover the secret of Venetian glass	117
—— Vase	38
TACITUS.—Agrees with Pliny on the invention of glass	22
TELESCOPE.—Etymology	299
—— of Gregory	299
—— of Newton	299
—— of Herschel	301
—— Astronomical	295
—— Terrestrial	303
THEOPHILUS.—Quoted	82
THERMOMETER.—By whom invented	194
—— Manufacture of the tubes	196
—— Graduation	199

TABLE OF CONTENTS.

	PAGE
VASE of Strasbourg	38
—— Portland	175
VENICE.—Origin of the glass trade according to Carlo Marin	42
—— Assumes the monopoly	43
—— Tyranny of the Council of Ten	44
—— History of Angelo Beroviero	46
—— To whom the idea of exportation was due	47
—— Singular shapes of Venetian glasses	147
—— Its glass sprinkled with gold	160
VERSAILLES.—Gallerie des Glaces	119
VESTALS.—Used metallic mirrors	91
VIDAORE (ANDREA).—Improves the manufacture of false pearls	245
VOCABULARY of terms used in glass manufacture	71
WINCKELMANN.—Quoted	77
WILKINSON (SIR GARDNER).—Quoted	25
WINDOW GLASS.—History	77
—— Pompeian	78
—— Rarity in 16th and 17th century	80
—— What was substituted for them	80
—— Manufacture	84
—— Why they were long so small	87
—— Robinet's invention	87
—— Fluted	88

LIST OF ILLUSTRATIONS.

	PAGE.
THEBAN GLASS-MAKERS.	24, 25
BEAD OF A ROYAL NECKLACE	26
INSCRIPTION IN HIEROGLYPHICS	26
ROMAN GLASS	29, 35, 39
STRASBOURG VASE	38
GLASS FURNACE	74
POTS	75
BLOWING OF SHEET GLASS	85
EGYPTIAN MIRRORS	90
MIRROR OF MARIE DE MEDICI	99
ITALIAN MIRROR WITH A FRAME OF CARVED WOOD	103
IVORY BOX CONTAINING A MIRROR	107, 109
MIRROR OF HENRY III.	113
MANUFACTURE OF BOTTLES	129
MOULD FOR CLARET BOTTLES	131
VENETIAN BOTTLE	133
JUG (Glass-works of Clichy)	135, 137
GERMAN WIEDERKOMMEN	143
VENETIAN GLASS	148, 149, 152, 155
GLASSES (Crystal Works of Clichy)	153
FRENCH GLASS OF THE 16TH CENTURY	157
VENETIAN GLASS SPRINKLED WITH GOLD	160
BOHEMIAN GLASS	167
ENGRAVED FLAGON	169
PORTLAND VASE	177
VENETIAN FROSTED GLASS	183
SPUN GLASS	187
MANUFACTURE OF THERMOMETERS	196, 198, 199

LIST OF ILLUSTRATIONS.

	PAGE.
EGYPTIAN BREASTPLATE	203
VENETIAN VASE	223
SPECIMEN OF FILIGREE CANES	227
SOLAR SPECTRUM	262
RECOMPOSITION OF LIGHT	264
FURNACE FOR OPTICAL GLASSES	266
MANUFACTURE OF CROWN GLASS	269
BASIN AND BALL	272
SIMPLE MICROSCOPE	277
COMPOUND MICROSCOPE	279
PROGRESS OF LUMINOUS RAYS	280
MICROMETER	282
CAMERA LUCIDA	287
MAGIC LANTERN	289
SOLAR MICROSCOPE	291
PHOTO-ELECTRIC MICROSCOPE	293
ASTRONOMICAL TELESCOPE	295, 297
GREGORIAN TELESCOPE	300
OPERA GLASS	307
BINOCULAR GLASS	307
LIGHT-HOUSE LANTERN	311

PREFACE.

Among the discoveries due to chance and perfected by man's intellect, the invention of Glass is certainly one of the most important.

Besides the fact that Glass satisfies a considerable number of our most ordinary wants, it is also to its power that we must attribute in a great degree the ever-progressive march of science; and indeed it is by multiplying indefinitely the strength of man's organ of sight, that Glass lays bare the most hidden works of creation to his investigation.

Thanks to its aid, there are no longer any impenetrable mysteries for science; by degrees everything is seen, studied, explained, and analyzed. Two examples, taken from the extremes of creation, the infinitely great and imperceptibly small, will sufficiently prove this. The Telescope, which brings the heavenly bodies within the range of the astronomer's study; and the Microscope, which may be said to be still more useful, inasmuch as it is the light of all natural science, and the source of the most curious and important discoveries. It shows us much, the existence of which we did not even suspect; it opens a new world before us; the most imperceptible atom of nature assumes a body and increases so much in size, that where there was apparently nothing we see myriads of beings.

Both these examples certainly deserve the name of Marvels; but they are not the only wonders worked by Glass, which obeys every wish of man, and lends itself to all his wants and fancies.

Does not our every-day life profit by its benefits? Light is admitted to our houses by means of glass, which yet excludes the inclemencies of the seasons; our forms are reproduced in looking-glasses; glass lustres double the lights in a chandelier by their numerous reflections; and if we glance into a dining-room, glass is still before us in the shape of decanters and drinking-glasses of pure and graceful shapes.

So many different appliances are none the less marvellous because we are accustomed to see them every day, and they do not the less deserve to have each of them their story told. This is the work we have undertaken.

If, notwithstanding our researches, and all the care we have taken in their classification, the reader still finds something forgotten, or even some errors (and we are far from thinking our work is exempt from them), he must kindly forgive them in consideration of all that our subject embraces.

The fear which obliges us to this avowal will surprise no one when we say that one of the most learned men of our period, M. Péligot, treating the question of Glass under its different chemical and practical forms, says to his readers: " I am under no illusion as to the imperfections of my work,* but I hope that allowance will be made for the difficulties found in collecting the scattered documents on glass working, a manufacture which lives in tradition, which avoids publicity, and on which, if I except the articles in encyclopædias and chemical treatises, no complete work has been attempted for more than a century and a half."

If, through an excess of modesty, M. Péligot claims the reader's indulgence for himself, who has certainly less need of it than any one else, how can we, at the commencement of this book, forbear to solicit a greater and more necessary indulgence ?

* *Da Douze leçons sur l'Art de la Verrerie.*

THE WONDERS OF GLASS-MAKING.

CHAPTER I.

INTRODUCTION.

Few questions have been more discussed than that of the origin of glass. Are we indebted for it to Phœnicia, Phrygia, Thebes, or Sidon? Or, going back into ages long before the foundation of these kingdoms, must its invention, as many writers maintain, be fixed at a period when men, having discovered fire and submitted to its action natural bodies, either separately or together, observed, among other phenomena, the vitrifaction of certain masses?

To admit this last opinion is to recognize as the inventor Tubal-Cain,[*] son of Lamech and Zillah, who, according to tradition, was the eighth man after Adam, and who is mentioned in Genesis iv. 22 as "an instructor of every artificer in brass and iron."

This acknowledged antiquity was certainly suffi-

[*] Born in the year of the world 130 (3870 B.C.), which would carry the discovery of glass back 5739 years.

ciently venerable to content the most scrupulous when M. Reimann, a German *savant*, maintained that the translation from the Hebrew was defective, and that it should be read that Tubal-Cain had only taught the engraving on copper and on iron.

This reading, which only represents the son of Lamech and Zillah as an artist embellishing iron and bronze worked by others before his time, would oblige us to go back still further in order to find the first smelter of metals, and in the attempt to obtain such a problematic result, we should not have left to us more than a hundred years to the commencement of the world. We, therefore, request the permission of our readers to quit these suppositions, and to come as quickly as possible to facts attested by actual remains, for after all this antediluvian erudition, we remain in utter ignorance as to the date of the discovery of glass.

Before, however, coming to the remains themselves, we must give our readers the account given by Pliny * of the accidental manner in which glass was discovered. "It is said," narrates the classic writer, " that some Phœnician merchants, having landed on

* Tacitus gives the same account as Pliny, but in a simpler manner, for leaving unexplained the process of melting employed, and entirely suppressing the mention of the cooking vessels, he merely states that some sand found at the mouth of the Belus, a river which flows into the sea of Judæa, when mixed with nitre and melted by fire, produced glass.

The shore, though of moderate extent, still affords an inexhaustible supply of sand.

the coast of Palestine, near the mouth of the river Belus, were preparing for their repast, and not finding any stones on which to place their pots, took some cakes of nitre from their cargo for that purpose. The nitre being thus submitted to the action of fire, with the sand on the shore, they together produced transparent streams of an unknown fluid, and such was the origin of glass."

This opinion with some variation is repeated on the authority of Flavius Josephus, by Palissy, in his *Traité des eaux et fontaines* (p. 156).

" Some say that the children of Israel, having set fire to some forest, the fire was so fierce that it heated the nitre with the sand, so as to make them melt and run down the slopes of the hills; and that thenceforward they sought to produce artificially what had been effected by accident in making glass."

The account, which is moreover given by Pliny on hearsay only, and which he is therefore unable to certify, has found, and still finds, a great number of disbelievers among chemists, who cannot understand, or who rather explicitly deny that at any period it was possible to liquefy in the open air substances which, in our day and with our improved processes, can only be fused by means of furnaces constructed expressly for the purpose, and which concentrate a heat of 1000° to 1500° centigrade (Fahr. 1832° to 2732°).

It is then impossible for us to decide either the scientific question or the claim to prior invention among the productions (found in great numbers in our museums) that, while dating back to an extremely early epoch, bear no indication of the place or date of their manufacture, which alone could enable us to range them in chronological order.

We will therefore merely begin with those objects which, from the place of their discovery or from the inscriptions they bear, belong, according to our actual knowledge, to remote antiquity.

Reference will first be made to the Theban glass-makers represented in the paintings on the tombs of Beni-Hassan, which are supposed to date about two thousand years before the Christian era. Certain writers even believe them to have been executed during the reign of Ousertasen I. (3500 B.C.).

The accompanying illustration (Fig. 1) represents a Theban crouching at the foot of a furnace, and apparently taking from it the molten glass. The next (Fig. 2) shows two others seated on the ground, each holding a blow-pipe, very similar in all respects to those used at the present day. At the end of each of the tubes, which are turned towards a fire, is some glass which the men are beginning to blow. And in the third illustration are two glass-makers, also with blow-pipes, blowing a vase, the mouth of which touches the ground.

Fig. 1.—Theban Glass-maker.

Such an early date (3500 B.C.) cannot be admitted altogether without question, since it is uncertain whether the paintings were executed during the reign of Ousertasen I. or his successors.

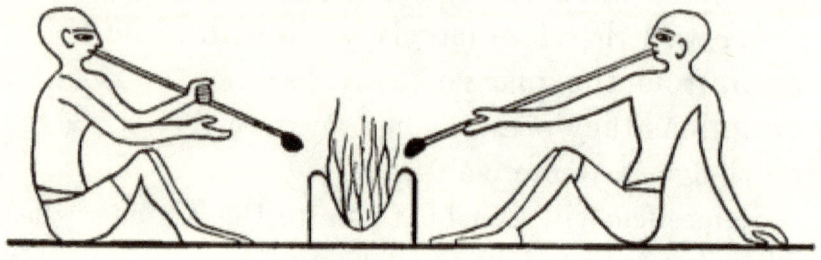

Fig. 2.—Theban Glass-makers.

While stating authoritatively that glass-making was practised at Thebes, let us take another example which will be indisputable, for the necklace bead of

Fig. 3.—Theban Glass-makers.

which we give an illustration (Fig. 4) bears the name of the queen for whom it was made, and, consequently, the date of its fabrication. This glass bead was found at Thebes, by Captain Hervey of the Royal Marines; and a description of it has been given by Sir Gardner Wilkinson,* in which he states that this

* 'The Manners and Customs of the Ancient Egyptians.' Vol. iii. p. 88. Ed. 1847.

"moulded" bead of very advanced art bears the hieroglyphic legend of the queen impressed upon it in sunken characters.

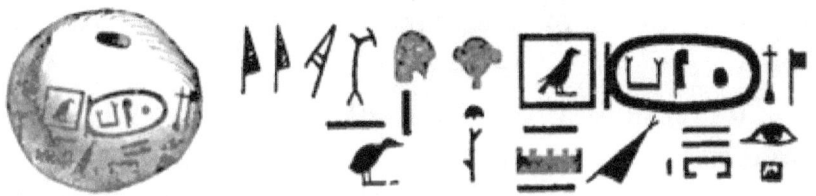

Fig. 4.—Bead of a Royal Necklace.

Fig. 5.—Inscription in Hieroglyphics.

This legend round the aa has in the engraving been extended, so as to enable the reader to see the whole of it at once. For the translation of it we are indebted to M. Théodulfe Devéria, son of the celebrated Achille Devéria, already well-known in the scientific world for his ability in deciphering hieroglyphics.

We give his own words:

"Only the first line of this legend is legible. It may be translated without difficulty as follows:— 'The good goddess (i.e., the queen) Ra-ma-ka, the loved of Athor, protectress of Thebes.' Ra-ma-ka was the first name of the Queen Hatasou, the wife of Thoutmes III., who reigned in the eighteenth dynasty (1500 B.C., according to the chronology of Brugsch)."

Here then we see Thebes with this manufacture without any precise date, but exhibiting an advanced art 3367 years ago.

Thebes, as we shall shortly see, was not the only

town in Egypt which practised with success the manufacture of glass; for Pliny boasts of the glass-manufactures of Sidon, and Herodotus and Theophrastus sing the praises of the marvellous productions of the Tyrians.

The fame of these different manufactures in glass could not remain unknown to the Romans; accordingly, scarcely had Cæsar Augustus subdued Egypt (26 B.C.), than he ordered that glass should form part of the tribute to be imposed on the conquered.

This tax, far from having been, as one might have thought, a cause of ruin for Egypt, became a source of wealth to all her glass manufactories; for Rome, always eager of novelty, having patronised these new productions, the result was that the Egyptians devoted themselves to a very large export trade, of which they preserved the monopoly until the reign of Tiberius (14 A.D.), at which period, according to Pliny, this industry began to be cultivated at Rome.

The Romans, gifted with a quick intelligence, by employing the processes used in Egypt, taught them by Egyptian artists allured to Rome, or by pupils who had been sent to their new province, made such rapid progress that in a short time their productions rivalled the most beautiful specimens which the Egyptians had formerly brought them, both in shape, color, and the cutting of the glass.

A single quotation from Pliny (Book xxxvi. chap. 24) will at once make us appreciate the immense importance of the Roman glass manufactures, and give us an idea of the luxury which was displayed by one Scaurus on being appointed to the post of ædile.

"I will not permit, however, these two Caiuses, or two Neros, to enjoy this glory even, such as it is; for I will prove that these extravagant follies of theirs have been surpassed, in the use that was made of his wealth by M. Scaurus, a private citizen. Indeed, I am by no means certain that it was not the ædileship of this personage that inflicted the first great blow upon the public manners, and that Sylla was not guilty of a greater crime in giving such unlimited power to his stepson, than in the proscription of so many thousands. During his ædileship, and only for the temporary purposes of a few days, Scaurus executed the greatest work that has ever been made by the hands of man, even when intended to be of everlasting duration; his Theatre, I mean. This building consisted of three storeys, supported upon three hundred and sixty columns; and this, too, in a city which had not allowed without some censure one of its greatest citizens to erect six pillars of Hymettian marble. The ground-story was of marble, the second of glass, a species of luxury which ever since that time has been quite unheard of, and the highest of gilded wood. The lowermost columns, as previously stated, were eight and thirty feet in height; and, placed between these columns, as already mentioned, were brazen statues, three thousand in number. The area of this theatre afforded accommodation for eighty thousand spectators; and yet the Theatre of Pom-

Fig. 6.—Roman Glass.

CALIFORNIA

peius, after the City had so greatly increased, and the inhabitants had become so vastly more numerous, was considered abundantly large with its sittings for forty thousand only. The rest of the fittings of it, what with Attalic vestments, pictures, and other stage properties, were of such enormous value that, after Scaurus had had conveyed to his Tusculan villa such parts thereof as were not required for the enjoyment of his daily luxuries, the loss was no less than one hundred millions of sesterces, when the villa was burnt by his servants in a spirit of revenge."

This sum is equivalent to eight hundred and forty thousand pounds sterling, or $4,200,000 in gold.

It would be wrong to infer from the folly of Scaurus that the Roman glass-makers manufactured such objects as these only; for being both artists and men of commerce, if they made objects of art (and of this we will presently give a proof), they never forgot that industry can only live on condition that its products, appealing to all, supply a general want. The immense quantity of glass objects which are found in Roman tombs, and of which we are going to speak, prove that glass for ordinary use was very common in Rome.

To support this assertion we will give our readers a complete inventory, in three distinct categories, of the glass objects which were discovered in 1837, in a Roman tomb at Baccalcone.

We will first speak of those which, from being found in all tombs, appear to be the result of a cus tom then general, and afterwards of those objects in daily use which were only left in the tombs at the pleasure of the relations, who placed with the dead the objects he had used or for which he had a particular regard.

Every one knows that this veneration for tokens of remembrance still exists at the present time. The following extract from " Des coutumes et cérémonies observées par les Romains," * shows us the use of each of these different objects.

"In order to burn the body, a funeral pile was erected in the shape of an altar, and composed of very combustible wood. Around this was placed some cypress-wood. The body, sprinkled with the most precious perfumes (Fig. 6, bottles Nos. 2, 3, 7, 8, 9), was then placed on the pile, and the nearest relations of the deceased, turning their faces away, set fire to it. The most costly garments of the dead and his weapons were also thrown upon it; the relations cut their hair and threw it on the funeral pile. Whilst the body was burning, human blood was spilled before the pile (cup No. 4). This appeased, as they believed, the manes of the deceased. When the body was consumed, the flames were extinguished with wine (vase No. 5), and the relations enclosed the bones and ashes in an urn (No. 1), in which were mingled flowers and odoriferous liquid perfumes."

We think that the object represented by No. 6,

* Translated from the Latin of Nieupoort, by the Abbé Desfontaines. Paris, Nyon, 1740, p. 108.

and of which we have not yet spoken, is only a bottle representing a bird. Vessels of this shape are often met with.

Let us leave this sad spectacle for a much more cheerful subject—a Roman lady's toilet. There we shall find proof that, if the ancients have endowed us with a great number of wonders, they have been well avenged by transmitting to their descendants that fashion, now, alas! too common, which in spite of all the skill of the painter, absolutely deceives only the person who uses it—that of painting the skin. Yes, readers, the Roman ladies of the Decadence painted themselves, and it even appears that they were perfect mistresses of the art. The first object which we will notice is a hollow colored glass ball (Fig 7, No. 1) which contained the paint, and the necessary adjunct of which is a twisted glass wand (No. 4), flattened at each end, which served to spread the color on the face.

As we do not pretend to maintain as a general assertion that the ancients have invented everything, we seize this opportunity of according to France the honor of having substituted a hare's foot for the glass wand. And this, as we are told by a person well skilled in the matter, is at the present time superseded by a little ball of very fine cotton wool.

We have previously said that Roman glass furnished a great many articles for domestic use. We do not indeed pretend that those which we offer to the reader represent the whole of them; but they will suffice to prove that the Romans possessed at least a great number similar to those which we use at the present time.

In plate 8, page 39, No. 1 represents an amphora with two handles, and beside it (No. 2) one of those amphoras without handles which were designated by Petronius *amphora vitrea* (glass amphora), and which, as we see, presents a great resemblance to our bottles.

Connected with the subject of bottles, let us next call the reader's attention to the fragment of a drinking glass (No. 3) which, broken as it is, offers a great similarity to those which we now use (see the chapters headed *Bottles* and *Drinking Glasses*). Near it is a jug (No. 4) with one handle, used, it is said, to contain preserved fruits, which were doubtless served in the dish (No. 5). When Gaul had fallen under the Roman power, the first care of the conqueror was to introduce into that country her laws, manners, and customs, as well as her different manufactures. Amongst these last, the only one which must now occupy us—the art of glass making—is certainly one of those which were the most widely diffused. In fact, the excavations made with so much care some years ago in the ancient provinces of France, have brought to light a very large quantity of glass objects, —similar as regards substance and mode of manufacture, as well as shape, to those found in the Roman tombs; so that one would be led to consider Rome as the only place of their manufacture, had not the discovery of an infinite number of Gallic glass-manufac-

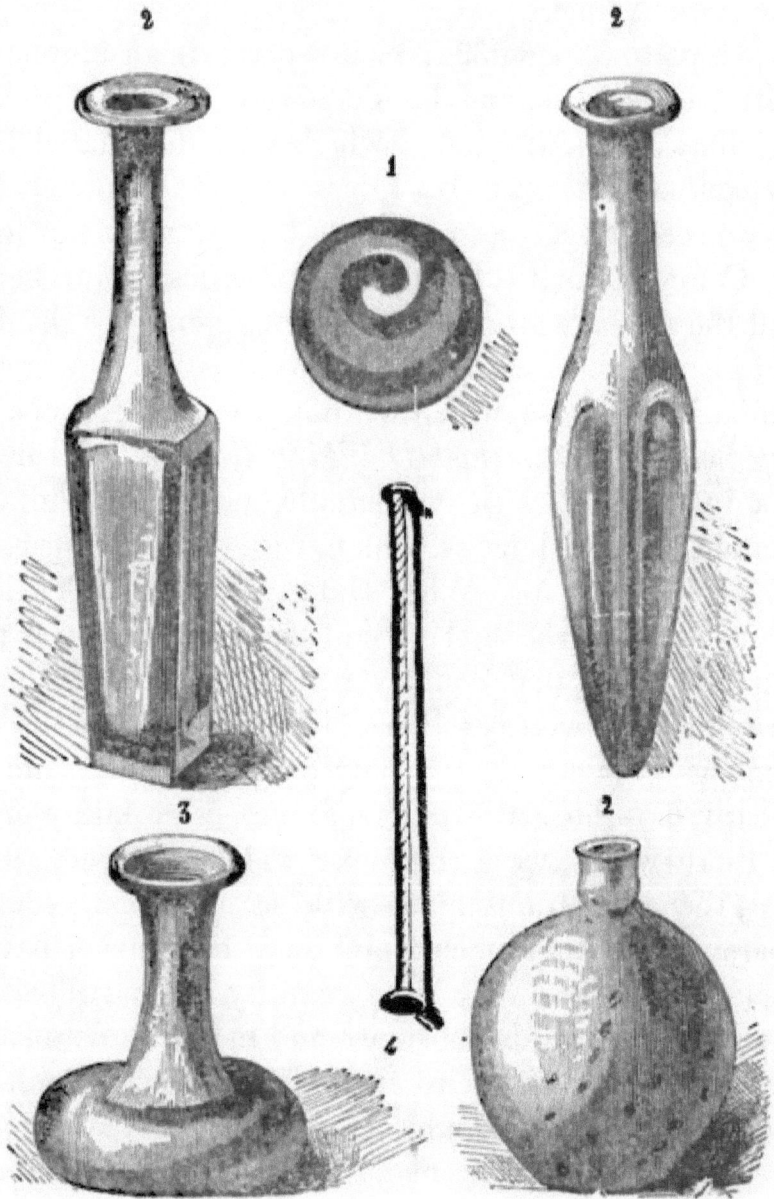

Fig. 7.—Roman Glass.

tures by the natives proved that the Gauls were at an early period great rivals to the Roman glass-makers (not only in common objects, but also in works of art). We will give one example only, the Strasbourg vase (Fig. 9), which, by the difficulty of its manufacture, indicates a very advanced state of art.

The following description of it is given by M. Schweighauser, librarian to the town of Strasbourg :—*

"The vase, surrounded with a kind of network of red-colored glass,† and bearing an inscription in green glass, was found in 1825, in a coffin, disinterred by chance near the glacis of Strasbourg, by a gardener. It has been placed by my care in the museum belonging to our public library, where it is admired by all who see it. It was broken by the clumsy curiosity of the man who found it, and a part of the inscription is missing. However, the name of MAXIMIANVS AVGVSTVS can be distinguished. This was without doubt MAXIMIANUS HERCULIUS,‡ who often dwelt amongst the Gauls, and whose medals are very frequently found in our district. This emperor had probably eceived the vase as a present,

---

* 'Notice sur quelques monuments gallo-romains du département du Bas-Rhin.' Vol. xvi. p. 95 des 'Mémoires de la Société royale des antiquaires de France.' 1842.

† By colored glass the writer evidently means colored in the mass, or enamelled.

‡ A Roman emperor who was born in Pannonia about the year 250, and died at Marseilles in 310.

and had given it away to some friend, who died in the vicinity of Argentoratum (Strasbourg), and with whom it was buried as a precious object."

Fig. 9.—The Strasbourg Vase.

The numerous glass-works, established both in Gaul and Spain, existed up to the period when, civilisation being driven back by the barbarians who carried fire and pillage into Rome, they fell, like every other industry, into such decay, that the processes of the manufacture were lost to the West.

Fig. 8.—Roman Glass.

It is said that nothing absolutely perishes, and the words are true as regards glass-making; for if it died in the West, it was revived in the East under Constantine I.,* who having transferred the seat of the empire to Byzantium (Constantinople), hastened to attract to himself the artists and workmen of the West, who found in that new empire aid and protection, and, moreover, an immense market for all kinds of industries, to such a degree that, in order to facilitate their export trade, the glass-makers were collected near the harbor. Theodosius II.† desiring to encourage this branch of commerce, even exempted the glass-makers from all personal taxes. With such protection, the art of glass-making could not but prosper; and its productions obtained such a reputation that they were offered as presents to the princes and kings of the West.

In spite of these successes attained by Byzantium, the time came when the West again resumed its old industry. Venice reclaimed it, and at her summons the East gave up, about the fourteenth century, the nearly exclusive monopoly which her glass-makers had extended over the West.

* Constantine I., surnamed the Great, a Roman emperor, the son of Constantius Chlorus and Helena, was born at Naissus in Upper Mœsia, A.D. 274, and died A.D. 337.

† Theodosius II., the son of Arcadius, a Roman emperor, born A.D. 399, and reigned from A.D. 408 to 450.

VENETIAN GLASS.

According to the Italian writers Carlo Marin *
and the Count Filiasi, the birth of Venetian glass-
making was nearly contemporary with the foundation
of the city, which is attributed, as is known, to the
emigration of some families from Aquileia and Pa-
dua, who fleeing from the armies of Attila, came and
took refuge on the islands of the lagoons about the
year 420.

While admitting the possibility of such an antiquity for the manufacture, we will pass to a better
known epoch, which will permit us to follow the art
in its progress to perfection.

The period we shall take for our starting point,
and which is certainly one of the most brilliant in the
history of the Venetian Republic, is that in which its
navy, rivalling those of Pisa and Genoa, after having
subdued the maritime towns of Istria and Dalmatia,
carried to Asia not only merchandise, but pilgrims to
the Holy Land and Crusaders on their way to fight
against the infidels.

In the year 330 Constantine I. had, as we have
said, attracted to the East the most famous artists of
the West, and Venice nine centuries afterwards sum-
moned in her turn Greek artists to come to her. It
is from this period, in fact (the end of the thirteenth

---

* Carlo Marin, 'Storia civile e politica del commercio de' Vene-
ziani.'

century), that the records of the republic prove both the importance of the numerous glass-works existing in Venice, and the interest which she attached to that art; such an interest that, as Carlo Marin said, " she loved it as the apple of her eye."

Is this love, so much admired and so much extolled by certain writers, as disinterested as they have been pleased to say? or rather does it not resemble that of a certain Persian prince, who whenever he took a fancy to any one, had him chained up so that he could not leave the palace?

It is this question which we are going to examine, hoping to prove in a very few words that there is justice in this comparison between the Persian prince and the Venetian republic.

Venice being at that time the only place where objects in glass were manufactured, every foreign country was forced to apply to her; and thanks to the numerous demands, as well as the continual and immense exportations, of which a fellow-citizen gave the idea, foreign gold accumulated at Venice. This kind of commerce already offered immense advantages to this eminently commercial republic; it was only necessary to find means to assure them for the future; so it was to attain this end, and of course for love of *the glass-makers*, that the chief council ordered it to be proclaimed that it would punish with confiscation any one who exported from Venice, not manufactured articles which were to be turned into gold for her advantage, but the primary materials of which glass is composed, receipts for its manufacture, and even broken glass; in one word, everything which might enable other countries to enter into competition with Venice in the least degree. This first step had hardly been taken towards this monopoly, when the chief council, which appears not to have had an unlimited confidence in the oath sworn by the glass-makers with regard to this law, promulgated a second law (A.D. 1289), which taking as a pretext the probable fires which would be occasioned by the numerous furnaces of the glass-makers (the number of which had already greatly increased), ordered them to quit Venice, and establish themselves on the little island of Murano, which is only separated from the city by a narrow strip of sea.

It will be easily understood that from this concentration of all the glass-makers there naturally resulted a system of espionage, which rendered the task of the police much easier, and supported in a still more certain manner the monopoly which the republic strove to maintain. Since we are on the question of monopoly, we think that we could not make its importance better understood than by placing before our readers a document which, emanating from the Council of Ten, will enable them to judge for themselves of the severity—we might even say the infamy—of a decree which, not content with punishing the innocent in order to reach the guilty, did not even shrink from assassination. This document, which is to be found in the "Histoire de la République de Venise," by M. Daru, is given by M. J. Labarte as follows:—*

"On the 13th February, 1490, the supervision of the manufactories in Murano was confided to the chief of the Council of Ten, and on the 27th October, 1547, the council reserved to itself the right of watching over the factories, in order to prevent the art of glass-making from passing into foreign countries." These precautions, however, not appearing sufficient to the Council of Ten, the State Inquisition, in the twenty-sixth article of its Statutes, announced the following decision:—

"If a workman carries his art into a foreign country, to the detriment of the Republic, an order to return will be sent to him.

"If he does not obey, his nearest relations will be put in prison.

"If in spite of the imprisonment of his relations he should persist in remaining abroad, an emissary will be charged to kill him."

In order to prove that this law did not stop at simple intimidation, M. Daru adds that in a document in the records of the foreign affairs, there are to be found two cases of assassination, of which the victims were workmen whom the Emperor Leopold had attracted to Germany.

To these documents of unimpeachable authenticity, we may add some others of a much more re-

* Histoire des arts industriels au moyen âge et à l'époque de la Renaissance,' vol. iv. p. 562.

cent date, such as the decrees of the High Council of the 22nd March and the 13th April, 1762, which not only confirmed the provisions previously made, but which added fresh rigor to the old laws, both against the workmen who established themselves in a foreign country, and against those who divulged the secret of the manufacture. We shall then have a precise idea of the pretended protection afforded to the glass-makers of Murano by the Venetian Republic.

We think that we have presented the question of the monopoly in its true light. Now we will go back and consider the art, so to speak, from its artistic beginning at Venice.

Amongst the most illustrious glass-makers we must place in the first rank Angelo Beroviero (15th century), who is justly regarded as having made the greatest step in the art of glass-making, aided, however, by Paolo Godi da Pergola, a celebrated Venetian chemist, who gave him a number of receipts for the coloring of glass. These receipts were of such importance to Beroviero, who alone possessed them, that for fear doubtless lest his memory should deceive him, he had them all carefully written in a manuscript, which he kept hidden from every one.

"One is never betrayed except by one's friends," says an old proverb, and we are about to give a fresh proof of its sad truth.

Beroviero had a daughter named Marietta, and employed a young man as a workman named Giorgio, or rather "il Ballerino," as he was called, in consequence of a deformity in his feet; a deformity, says tradition, which made his whole person so ungainly, that it was to his simple and candid look that he must have owed his being accepted by Beroviero, who was nearly as suspicious as the Republic. Whether Giorgio fell in love with the young Marietta, or whether Marietta shut her eyes to the deformity of the young workman, the legend does not say: all that we are told is that *il Ballerino* one day seized upon the manuscript volume, which it appears was confided to the care of Marietta, and copied the whole of it.

Having finished this work, Giorgio, armed with the second copy, the existence of which the over-confident Beroviero was far from suspecting, demanded and obtained, in place of the enormous price he should get by the sale of the book, the hand of Marietta, together with a handsome dowry, by the aid of which he constructed a furnace that brought him considerable gains.

We have previously spoken of a certain Venetian who, by the accounts which he gave to his fellow glassmakers, largely increased the exportation of a portion of the glass manufactures generally, but especially of that class which we will designate by the name of glass-jewellery, such as trinkets, false pearls, imitation precious stones, &c. In connection with this subject we have another legend, which is the more probable as the facts narrated are entirely in accordance with the manners of the Venetians, who, as is known, were born traders.

There were at Venice, about the year 1250, two brothers, one named Matteo Polo and the other Nicolo. Both were navigators, or rather perhaps merchants passing their lives in visiting the most commercial cities of those distant lands which at that time were commonly known as the barbarian countries.

Nicolo had a son who, following the adventurous life of his father and his uncle, became that illustrious Marco Polo,* who after attaching himself (1271) to the service of Kublai Khan, became governor of the provinces under the dominion of that prince.

On his return to Venice (1295) Marco hastened to inform his fellow-citizens, who were dauntless mariners, as well as enterprising merchants, not only of the manners but also of the taste of the people of Tartary, India, and China, for false pearls and imitation gems. Nothing more was required to excite the inventive mind of the Venetians. Thus whilst Dominico Miotti endowed Venice with the invention of blowing false pearls, which had been lost for many centuries, Christopher Briani on his side revived an art formerly carried to great perfection, the production of colored glass and *aventurine*.

Such efforts necessarily brought their reward, and it is to the pearls and colored glass in imitation of precious stones that Venice owed in a great part the wealth which she gathered from both hemispheres.

* A celebrated Venetian traveller who was born about 1250, and died in 1323.

GERMAN GLASS.

In spite of the rigorous and tyrannical ordinances of the Venetian authorities, of which we have given an idea, light began at length to dawn upon other countries; and Germany, the first to shake off the monopoly which weighed on her as well as on all the other states, began to produce objects in glass not resembling those of Murano in shape and ornament, but so dissimilar that we may say that she created a new industry. In fact, leaving to Venice her fine and light filigree work, Germany only decorated her glasses with paintings in enamel, generally representing coats of arms (see page 143).

The most ancient vase, which represents the coat of arms of the Elector Palatine, bears the date of 1553. It is exhibited in the Kunstkammer of Berlin.

Amongst the artists in glass-making who were the most renowned in Germany, were Johann Schaper of Nuremberg (1661 to 1666), H. Benchert (1677), Johann Keyll (1675), and the Saxon chemist, Kunkel (died 1702), to whom Germany is indebted for numerous receipts for the coloring of glass, and among others for that of the beautiful ruby red.

BOHEMIAN GLASS.

The industrial start was given in the West, for to Germany succeeded Bohemia, which entered the industrial lists not only with glass of much greater clearness than that of the manufacturers of Italy and

Germany, but also with a decorative system up to that time unknown—engraving on glass—invented it is believed about 1609, by Gaspar Lehmann, and continued by his pupil George Schwanhard. The taste, or rather the fashion, which caused the Venetian and German glass-manufactures to be abandoned for the engraved glass of Bohemia, became so widely spread in the seventeenth century, that Bohemian engravers decorated certain Venetian objects of the fifteenth and sixteenth centuries with engravings executed either by the lathe or by the diamond. This union of two industries, separated by more than a century, and moreover united on the same objects, gives rise to a great uncertainty as to their origin.

As this question interests numerous amateurs at the present time, we will quote the words of M. J. Labarte,[*] who in this matter is one of the *savans* whose opinion is of the greatest weight.

"There is in the Musée de Cluny a glass with a high stem, engraved with a full-length portrait of the Prince Frederick of Nassau,[†] with a German inscription. There is also another glass bearing the Spanish arms; a goblet on which is represented a hunting scene, with a Dutch inscription, and the date 1664; and a large glass with the arms of the seven United

---

[*] See the work before mentioned, 'Histoire des Arts industriels,' &c., vol. iv., p. 594.

[†] Henry Frederick of Nassau, the Prince of Orange, succeeded his brother Maurice, A.D. 1625, as chief of the Republic. He died A.D. 1647.

Provinces. All these engravings are made by the diamond."

These Venetian vases, which were not engraved until more than a century after their manufacture, must not, therefore, be taken for Bohemian glass.

Bohemian glass having numerous partizans in Europe, we think it would be agreeable to our readers to learn the opinion of M. Godard, manager of the manufactory at Baccarat.*

" The great manufacture of Bohemia is of glass, but it is glass which, while produced at a very low price, is white and clear enough to make it a formidable rival both to the glass and crystal of other countries.

" The greater part of the Bohemian glass factories have been established for the sole purpose of utilizing the woods, which would have no value were it not for the introduction of this industry. It is for the same reason that a certain number of glass factories and furnaces were established in France about one hundred or one hundred and fifty years ago, in the middle of the forest districts. But the increasing wealth of the country has multiplied the wants and developed these industries to such a degree, that the woods have become much sought after, and very dear. In Bohemia, on the contrary, the increase of wealth has been slower by far; the people have remained poor and without requirements, or without the means of

---

* ' Extract from the Inquiry into the Treaty of Commerce with England,' 1861. ' Imprimerie Impériale,' p. 558.

satisfying them; the woods therefore are still nearly without value; and the spirited, skilful, and intelligent Bohemian workman receives wages which can scarcely be realised by a resident in France, and the smallness of which is in all cases to be deplored.*

"There being hardly any consumption of glass in Bohemia, the country exports nearly all its products to the richer provinces of Austria, and to all Germany, to Switzerland, Italy, the East, Russia, America, &c.

"This industry has become quite popular in the country, where it guarantees to a considerable part of the population an occupation which does not make them rich, but helps to keep them from want, and at the same time procures a revenue for the large landowners by the use of their woods.

"These numerous establishments, of quite a rustic construction, generally placed in the middle of the forests, produce ordinary glass wares, objects destined to be highly worked or richly engraved, and colored glasses, which are decorated with gilding and paintings. Long experience in the manufacture of colored glass has made these workmen most skilful in this branch, and they are guided in case of need by the advice of men of information who have made a pro-

---

* In France the wages of a glass-maker cannot be estimated at less than four or five francs a day, and those of an engraver at less than six to ten francs; while in Bohemia one to two francs a day is the maximum. Since this was written the wages of the French glass-makers have been increased.

fession of the search after and sale of processes and improvements in glass-making; and rich lords advance the necessary capital, when it is required, in order to ensure the success of the manufactories established on their property.*

"Glass-cutting and lustre-making constitute special trades, carried on in huts on small streams, with wheels of the simplest construction.

"The engraving, gilding, and painting also form separate trades, which are all exercised with the same parsimony in the price of the workmanship.

"Finally, all these products are collected by commercial houses, which distribute them among the various markets.

"It is difficult to compare these products with ours as regards ordinary articles. The material is not the same. The Bohemian glass is pure, white, light, and agreeable to the hand. It has not the brilliancy of our crystal, and it is liable to turn yellow with time. Bohemia has preserved its shapes, which entirely differ from ours,† and which (perhaps because they are foreign) are appreciated by certain purchasers to such a degree that we are sometimes obliged to imitate them.

"Its process of manufacture differs most widely

---

* The same has happened in France. See the chapter on 'Gentlemen Glass-makers," page 6'.

† "Certain glass-works imitate in form and moulding the manufacture of Bohemia, such as the establishment of Valerysthal and some of the glass-works of Lorraine."

from that of other countries. In order to facilitate and shorten the work of the furnaces, the rims of the goblets, glasses with stems, &c., are cut with the cutter's wheel which, in England, Belgium, and France are cut with the glass-maker's shears; and the workmen having been long accustomed to this kind of work, have acquired a talent which cannot be found among any other nation for producing articles *à calotte*, that is to say, articles of which the top is taken off by the cutter instead of being opened by the glass-blower. These edges which are cut are not so well rounded, are less agreeable for use, and more likely to get chipped, than those which are formed by heat. But they have a neater and more satisfactory look to the eye, the objects are more even, the workman being freed from the care which he is obliged to take in order to prevent breaking them when opening them with his nippers. The majority of the purchasers prefer our edges, but it is easy to get accustomed to the Bohemian edges, which do not prevent the sale of the articles. But the great advantage of the manufacturers of Bohemia is the low price at which they can produce ware.

"There is among the fancy articles and colored glasses of Bohemia an originality which is not always in accordance with good taste, but which is valued and sought after by purchasers on account of its strangeness. It is Bohemia which has given birth to that kind of product, which agrees more with the German taste than with the French; and she has the right of seniority over us, an advantage which is so precious and so important in commerce.

"The productions of that country are less finished in detail than ours; the defective objects are put up for sale with the others; the mouths of bottles and other like objects are made with a carelessness which would not be tolerated in France. With these defects, which, while they would cause our articles to be rejected, are accepted as inherent to the Bohemian articles, these productions have a brilliancy, richness, and originality, which charm all the more as they are at the same time very moderate in price.

"Although in competition with Bohemia we sell colored crystals to foreign countries, and although the particular qualities of our manufacture are esteemed there, if our frontiers were opened to the glass wares of that country, considerable quantities of them would inevitably enter. Perhaps this taste would be extinguished in a few years, and the preference which we endeavor to merit would be given to us; but till then we should experience a considerable prejudice."

Since we are visiting foreign countries, although very rapidly, we will not now stop at France without saying something about the glass manufactures of Belgium and England. An anonymous writer, but a very competent one, shall treat of those of Belgium, leaving Messrs. Chance Brothers, of Birmingham, to speak to us of the glass-works of England.*

* 'Extract from the Inquiry into the Treaty of Commerce with England, 1861.' 'Imprimerie Impériale,' pp. 551–596.

BELGIAN GLASS.

"The organization and condition of Belgian glass-works resemble those of France much more than any other.

"This manufacture is carried on in Belgium in establishments erected on a large scale. Baccarat was originally a colony of a Belgian glass manufactory, which at the time of the separation of that country, in 1815, established a branch establishment in France, in order to preserve its French patronage.

"The principal advantage of the position of the Belgian glass-works is that they are placed over the coal mines of that country, which rival those of England; and that the lead which is extracted from the mines, like their coal, is not subject to expense of carriage nor payment of duty.

"The Belgians are especially to be feared on account of a manufacture of demi-crystal, which is not carried on in France, and in which they imitate all the shapes of our common crystals, at about the same price as glass.

"It is in this kind of production, intermediate between crystal properly so called and glass, that they are very skilful, which enables them to export great quantities as a substitute for crystal.

"Belgium greatly imitates in demi-crystal the French shapes in ordinary crystals, and offers them at a much lower price. They are generally not nearly so well executed as the French crystal. The system adopted in Belgium is to manufacture very quickly, so that it may be done very cheaply; and it is in this respect that it is formidable to the French glass manufacture."

ENGLISH GLASS.

The crystal trade in England is organized on a plan totally different from that pursued in France; in the former country the system resembles much more closely that followed in the manufacture of the ordinary glass-ware of France.

"Goblets made of common glass are not generally used in England, where the poorest as well as the richest families make use only of crystal, which material forms with them the substitute for our common glass.

"In this country there are about eighty crystal works, containing from one hundred to one hundred and twenty furnaces, and producing for the market crystal to the value of at least 1,600,000*l.* sterling, or $8,000,000 in gold. Not one half of this is required for home consumption; the remainder is destined for exportation, and prepared according to the requirements and customs of each of the nations among whom England carries on its extensive commerce.

"Most of these establishments are furnished in a very plain manner, like many of our own common glass-works, with little capital and few general expenses. They buy their first materials already prepared in special factories devoted to this work only, and to which the very numerous small crystal works form an important class of customers. A master assembles several hands; sometimes he is his own chief workman. He constructs a furnace near some of the inexhaustible coal mines of Newcastle or Birmingham; the first materials he buys on credit; a few moulds are ordered if he intends to undertake moulding; and thus he makes the crystal in ordinary use with scarcely any other expense than the price of fuel, the first materials, and the labor.

"If the crystal is to be cut, he sells it to those who undertake the cutting as a separate branch; that intended for exportation is sold to houses with a large foreign connection. Each factory, in consequence of its restricted limits compared with the importance of this trade in England, is thus enabled to confine itself to a particular branch of the manufacture, to acquire therein great dexterity, and be always certain of finding a market for its productions.

"This system does not offer to the producer great opportunities for acquiring profit, but it enables him to supply at very low prices, of which home competition and the necessity for selling do not always permit him to derive permanent advantage.

"There are in England more important and complete crystal works, especially such as are employed in the production of what are properly termed fancy crystals, in which articles they have acquired undoubted superiority; but English crystal ware is, however, quite as formidable in its small factories as in the great establishments."

We were about to close the article relating to England, when M. J. Labarte, who by his minute labors leaves nothing new to be said, tells us that the introduction of glass, the manufacture of which was unknown or neglected in England during the whole of the middle ages, had been introduced there by a certain Cornelius de Lannoy, who being invited to London by Queen Elizabeth, was the first to produce works in glass. According to the same scholar, it was during her reign that Jean Quarre, native of Antwerp, accompanied by workmen from his own country, established there a manufactory of the same kind as those already existing in France.

FRENCH GLASS-WARE.

To repeat here what we have said already, "that the Romans had established numerous glass-works in Gaul," would be doubtless to trace the origin of this art to a very remote period; but it must be admitted that if the manufacture of ordinary objects, common even in material and form, continued without interruption, it certainly was not the same with that which may be termed elaborate fancy glass-ware. We will mention, for example, the glass found at Strasbourg (page 37); and the excavations made in hundreds of places, especially in Normandy, present us for the most part only with forms which, being still in daily use, are repeated everywhere.

Let us come at once to the reign of Clotaire I.

(6th century), for it is here that we shall find one of the earliest notices of glass objects being used at the tables of the great. The proof exists in a letter written to Queen Radegonde, wife of Clotaire I., by Fortunatus, at that time bishop of Poitiers, in which he describes to her in the following terms a repast at which he had been present. " Each kind of food was served up on a different material. The meat on silver dishes; the vegetables on dishes of marble; the fowls on *glass dishes;* the fruit in painted baskets; and the milk in black earthenware pots shaped like a saucepan." Whilst fully allowing that this bill of fare cannot in luxury and profusion of dishes be compared with that of official banquets of which the newspapers much too often present us with a list as long as it is devoid of interest, yet it will be allowed that our ancestors even already were conversant with, and indulged in luxury at table.

From the sixth century let us pass to the fourteenth, and we shall then see how important the manufacture was five hundred years ago.

A document drawn up, on the glass-maker's privilege being accorded in 1338 by Humbert, Dauphin of Viennois, to a certain Guionet, who was about to follow his trade on the lands of the Dauphin, is interesting, not only as presenting us in succession with the objects of glass then in use, but still further, as showing us that my lord the Dauphin of Viennois did not confer his favors gratuitously.

" The Dauphin resigns to Guionet a part of the

forest of Chambarant, in order that he may establish a glass manufactory there, on condition that the latter supply *annually* for his house, one hundred dozen glasses in the form of bells, twelve dozen small glasses with wide tops, twenty dozen goblets or cups with feet, twelve amphoræ, thirty-six dozen chamber utensils, twelve large porringers, six dishes, six dishes without edges, twelve pots, twelve ewers, five small vessels called *gottefles*,* one dozen salt-cellars, twenty dozen lamps, six dozen chandeliers, one dozen large cups, one dozen small barrels, and lastly, six large casks for carrying wine."

A total for my lord of two thousand four hundred and thirty-five objects annually!

Does this very full list enumerate all the objects of glass used in the fourteenth century? One might be led to believe it; and yet we ask ourselves how our ancestors could, we will not say invent, but at least revive, certain of those glass trinkets which we frequently find in the Roman or Gallo-Roman tombs. When turning over the inventory of the departmental archives previous to 1790,† we found: "1592, to Florent Bougart, glass-maker, the sum of nine livres tournois, as payment for a small glass service which we sold to Henry, Dauphin of Viennois, for Mademoiselle Diane, his natural daughter."

* In spite of our researches we have been unable to discover the meaning of this word. Might it not be compared to glass in the form of a gondola, and described further on.

† Department of Seine-et-Marne, Series E., Titles of Families, E., 57 case.

The household of my lord the Dauphin of Viennois being amply furnished, and Mademoiselle Diane having her little service, nothing further remains for us but to refer the reader to the following pages, in which we shall give the origin (as far as possible), together with the mode of manufacturing the principal objects due to the glass-maker's art. But there is still one historical point to which we invite his attention, viz.: What is to be understood by a "gentleman glass-maker?"

GENTLEMEN GLASS-MAKERS.

According to the testimony of several authors, the general opinion admitted even in the present day is that formerly the mere trade of a glass-maker carried nobility with it; in a word, that every common glass-maker was ennobled by the mere fact of the nature of his trade.

Since such a prerogative—however impolitic it must have been, by doing the most flagrant and unmerited injustice to other important branches of industry—has been, and is still admitted as an historical fact, let us examine for a moment, as briefly as possible, on what ground this nobility rests, if it ever existed, and what could have been the origin of the error.

The two principal offenders, in our opinion, are a poet and a celebrated potter; the first,[*] by saying in his epigram against the poet Saint Amand—

[*] François Maynard, French poet, born at Toulouse in 1582, and died 1646.

> "Votre noblesse est mince,
> Car ce n'est pas d'un prince,
> Daphnis, que vous sortez;
> *Gentilhomme de verre,*
> Si vous tombez à terre,
> Adieu vos qualités;" *

and the second,† by employing this phrase in his immortal work: *L'Art de la verrerie est noble, et ceux qui y besongnent sont nobles.*‡

First, we undertake to establish that we are far from believing that a common glass-maker, more than any other manufacturer, ever merited or even ever obtained letters of nobility. Passing over these very rare exceptions, we are concerned here only with the corporation as a whole; in short, we shall endeavor to prove that, in France, the condition, the art even, if you like, of the glass-maker did never of necessity confer nobility on every one practising it.

As regards the two authorities antagonistic to our opinion, we give the text of one of numerous decrees which were issued against the plebeians on all occasions when they attempted to lay claim to nobility.

Here is the text of a decree of the *Cour des Aides*, at Paris, in September, 1597.

" . . . from the mere fact of working and trad-

---

* "Your nobility is puny, for you are not descended from a prince, Daphnis; *gentleman of glass*, should you fall to the ground, then farewell to your dignity."

† Bernard Palissy, born in the diocese of Agen, about 1510, died in Paris, 1589.

‡ Glass-making is a noble art, and those engaged in it are noble

ing in glass-ware, the glass-makers could not claim to have acquired nobility or right of exemption; nor, on the other hand, could the inhabitants of the locality assert that a nobleman was doing anything derogatory to his title by being a glass-maker."

From this enactment, repeated on each new attempt at usurpation, the natural consequence is, that the ordinary glass-maker did not acquire nobility, and that the nobleman did not forfeit his by devoting himself to the glass trade. A still more recent proof is found in Article 2 of the privilege granted to Du Noyer, by Louis XIV., 1665, to found the manufactory at St. Gobain: "Du Noyer may take as co-partners, even nobles and ecclesiastics, without it being derogatory to their nobility."

In support of our assertions, let us further cite an article of a decree issued by the Venetian senate, which certainly of all past governments is that which has accorded the greatest number of prerogatives to glass-makers

"The Senate decides that the marriage of a nobleman with the daughter of a glass-maker is contracted with the condition that the title of nobility be transmitted to their issue."

Nobility then is for the son of a noble; but as is seen, plebeian rank is still for the father-in-law.

The question of plebeians not having a right to nobility, as well as that of non-forfeiture for the noblemen being thus clearly settled, let us see what advantages accompanied the privileges generally conferred on noblemen, a favor of which we will shortly mention the cause.

These privileges are all mentioned in the letters-patent of November 24, 1598, conferring on Balthasar de Belleville, applying equally to him and his brother nobles, the permission to establish a glass-house in Normandy, and declaring them exempt from all excise, subsidies, imposts, customs, taxes on land, barriers, highways, tolls, commissions, *bandage, robinzge*, district, passage, and bridge and river dues.

In a word, the gentlemen glass-makers were then released from all existing imposts, which it is evident were rather numerous.

Was this favor—monopoly even, if you like—granted to nobility, prejudicial to plebeian glass-makers, as several writers have affirmed? We believe the contrary. Whilst allowing even that the nobles profited by the labor of the plebeian, it is to the nobleman alone that the common glass-makers owed their establishment and afterwards their fortune.

In order to discover the origin of this association, we must go back to that remote period when the nobleman readily sold his castle in order to support the dignity of his escutcheon in a tournament; or even to those warlike times when every subject hastened to place at his king's service the vassals on his domain, both great and small, armed and equipped at his own expense. We shall then see many of them returning to these domains covered equally with glory and debt, that is, ruined.

This condition, sad for any one, was disastrous to the nobility, for it is known that the law formally excluded them, and that under pain of forfeiture of title, from commerce, by which alone they could have retrieved their fortune.

However ardently the kings of France might wish to abolish a law which pressed heavily on those alone who had sacrificed everything in the service of their country, this desire was paralysed by the pride of the other nobles, who, still rich, compelled them to maintain in all its rigor a law in which, for fear of a subterfuge or oversight being found, all the trades then known were mentioned. At last this law shared the fate of everything not adapted to the times; and if it did not fall at once into disuse, a new importation, and consequently one not specified in the list of prohibited trades, glass-making, appeared, which allowed the kings, whilst still adhering to the ancient law, to profit by its silence relating to glass-making, and thus to open a resource as indispensable to the rising trade as to the re-establishment of the nobleman's fortune.

Such, in our opinion, is the real origin of the "gentlemen glass-makers," who, being nobles by birth, and no longer in dread of the law of forfeiture, in consideration of certain dues, delivered up their forests to the plebeian glass-makers. The latter, thanks to the nobles, found therein everything which they required, that is, space adapted to their trade, wood, without which they could not work, and still further, all the profits accruing from the exemptions, which being accorded to the lord alone, formed what in the present day would be known under the name of common capital (apport ou fonds social).

From the preceding then we conclude that, with some very rare exceptions, the title of "gentlemen glass-makers" was granted only to nobles who had the monopoly worked on their estate.

In the most rapid manner possible, we have noted the principal stages of the glass-making trade. Let us now fix our attention, not on all the objects produced by it, the list of which would be endless, but simply on those most in use, giving the origin of each, its mode of fabrication, as well as its successive stages of development.

CHAPTER II.

ON THE COMPOSITION OF GLASS.*

M. A. COCHIN, Member of the Institute, in his excellent work, entitled "La Manufacture de St. Gobain," † has treated the dry subject of the composition of glass in a manner at once so clear and terse, that for the benefit of the reader we request the author's permission to transcribe here his own words:—

"The theory of the manufacture of common glass and of glass mirrors is, like all nature's secrets, at once simple and beautiful.

"It has been the gracious will of the Creator that everything which is useful should at the same time be very abundant; but in order to make labor incumbent on us, He has been pleased to conceal His favors—it is for us to discover them. The materials required for the manufacture of glass are to be met

---

* Each kind of glass having its peculiar composition, in order to avoid unnecessary trouble, we have considered it best to notify each of them under the head of the object described. Thus, to learn the composition of window glass, mirrors, and all other objects, reference has only to be made to each of these articles. Flint-glass and crown-glass will be treated under the head of optics.

† Paris, Douniol, 1866, page 12.

with everywhere, but in an impure and mixed condition, like nearly all natural substances.

"*Silica* is the chief component of glass. Potash or soda and lime are mixed with the silica to obtain *window* and *plate glass;* add oxide of iron and you have *bottle glass;* substitute oxide of lead and you obtain *crystal;* replace it by oxide of tin and you produce *enamel.* The union of the fusible bases, potash, soda, and lead, with silicic acid, form compounds which are also fusible; the infusible bases, lime, alumina, magnesia, produce infusible compounds; but combined with fusible and infusible bases, the silicic acid forms multiple silicates which melt very readily. Plate-glass is precisely one of these mixtures of three elements. It is composed of silica, soda, and lime.*

"Silica exists everywhere. Rock crystal, sandstone, sand, flint, are composed of silica; it is also found in the ashes of plants, volcanic streams, and mineral springs. Sugar resembles glass, and this likeness is not deceptive. Melt the ashes of the sugar-cane, and you have glass: for with the silica, they contain both potash and lime.

* Nearly in this proportion:—
Silica... 73
Lime... 15
Soda... 12
                                                  ———
                                                  100

(Péligot, 'Douze leçons sur l'Art de la Verrerie,' page 58.)

"Calcareous substances compose perhaps one half of the crust of the globe. Lime is in our bones; it is also in vegetables and straw, in the human skeleton and common earth; it is found everywhere—even more widely distributed than silica.

"Soda also is found in nature. It has long been obtained by the combustion of certain marine plants; in the present day it is produced very easily by artificial means. Potash which may be employed instead of soda, is not less common and widely known; it exists in all ashes.

"Here then we have the key to all those profound mysteries of Murano, Bohemia, and St. Gobain. A mirror is a valuable object produced from the commonest materials. To assist the memory, let me thus sum up the preceding remarks. When warming your feet, if you look at yourself in the mirror, remember that the mirror which adorns your mantelpiece can be manufactured by the help of that same mantelpiece and the fireplace beneath: the stones furnish the silex, the ashes the potash, the marble lime, and the fire is the only mysterious agent required for the transformation. 'Glass,' according to the old saying, 'is the offspring of fire.'"

The materials being thus well known, we should have nothing further to add than to say by what means the fusion is obtained. Before doing so, however, we consider it indispensable to place before the reader a small vocabulary of the most ordinary words employed in glass-making; for like every science and art, so glass-making has its technical language, with which it is necessary to become acquainted for a thorough understanding of the work.

VOCABULARY.

Annealing.—This is the name given to one of the most important operations in the glass-making trade, for without annealing none of its productions could resist the least blow or change of temperature. To remove this defect, which necessarily results from cooling too suddenly, each of the objects when finished is placed, whilst still at red heat, in an especial furnace, where it is left to cool gradually. According to M. Péligot, the frequent breaking of lamp glasses, especially when used for the first time, must be attributed to imperfect annealing.

Blowing-iron.—A hollow iron tube. One of its extremities (that which the glass-blower holds in his hand) is furnished with a wooden covering. Of all the glass-blower's tools, the blowing-iron is doubtless the most indispensable. By its aid alone the blowing of the glass is performed, which, as will be seen, is the method employed in the manufacture of nearly every object of glass.

And as one may be convinced by referring to the plate (page 25) representing Theban glass-blowers, its use goes back to the most remote antiquity.

The blowing-iron measures from six to nine feet in length.

Boy.—Name indiscriminately given to the workman who assists the blower.

Colcars.—Furnaces for annealing the plate glass.

Fritting.—By this word, the object of which, as will be seen, plays a very important part in the fusion of glass, is meant the operation which consists of causing the vitreous substances to undergo a heat not only sufficiently powerful to remove any vapor and to consume any combustible substances therein, but still further to cause the fusion to begin.

The pots containing the frit are those which, placed at the sides of the furnace (see Fig. 10, page 74), undergo a less violent heat than the melting-pots which occupy the centre of the furnace.

Glass-house.—The workshop.

Ladle.—Of these there are two kinds: one serves to transfer the glass from a large pot to other smaller ones; the other to skim the glass while in fusion.

Marver.—Plate of cast or wrought iron, on which the blower prepares the glass.

Pouty.—A long rod of solid iron, serving either for drawing the glass out only, or twisting it to a fine thread. (See Filigree Glass Wares.) By drawing out the glass it is intended to obtain a much longer, and consequently a much finer thread than that from which it comes. To obtain this result, the boy applies his pouty to the glass whilst still in fusion and adhering to the blower's pipe, and going backwards, he draws the pouty with him, whilst the blower, who holds the tube in his hand, proceeds in a contrary direction, or even remains stationary.

Rake.—An iron instrument with the upper part

of wood, used for stirring the frit and vitreous matter in the pots.

Refining, see *Skimming*.

Shears.—They serve to cut the glass whilst still malleable.

Skimming.—The action of removing foreign matter floating on the glass. The operation is sometimes known under the name of *refining*.

Working-hole.—Name given to a kind of small windows which, opening and shutting at will, are placed over the pots in order that the workman may in succession introduce and withdraw the vitrifiable matter which he requires.

Now that we are acquainted with the materials from which glass is made,* and have learnt the signification of the technical words employed by glassmakers, we have only to enter their vast workshop, known among them by the name of *glass-house*.

THE FURNACES.

On entering the glass-house, the first thing which strikes us is the union of several buildings, assuming either a circular or rectangular form.

These are the furnaces, serving at once for the fritting and fusion.

Having to furnish a temperature between 1800 and 2700 degrees Fahrenheit, these furnaces are entirely constructed of fire-proof bricks, made of infusible clay and a cement obtained from the pulverisa-

* See page 69.

tion of old pots, which are themselves manufactured from the same clay. In France this is generally obtained at Forges-les-Eaux, Seine-Inférieure.

Fig. 10.—Glass Furnace.

Each furnace contains from eight to ten pots, which being placed on a stand, are by this means surrounded by the flames.

It is necessary for the manufacture that the workman should be enabled to gain constant access to the pots. For this purpose an opening called a working-hole is made in the furnace opposite each pot; by means of this the workman can not only fill his pots, and watch the fusion of the first materials, but also take the glass from them.

We may remark that the fire of the glass-maker's furnaces is never extinguished. When a pot is empty, fresh vitrifiable materials are at once introduced through the working-hole, so that the manufacture ceases only when the furnace is so worn that a new one must be constructed. A furnace lasts but one or two years at the most.

POTS.

The first material of which the pots are made is the same as that of the bricks of the furnace; we have therefore only to explain their manufacture.

Fig. 11.—Pots.

"The pots which serve for melting the glass," says the learned M. A. Péligot,* " vary in form and dimension, being either round, oval, or rectangular. For crystal made at the coal-mine, they are closed and shaped like a retort, with a very narrow neck. Their height varies from eighteen inches to three feet, and when baked, their sides are from two to three inches in thickness, and the bottom four inches. Large pots generally contain ten or twelve hundred-weight of melted glass.

After having remained from four to eight months in a room heated from 90 to 100 degrees Fahrenheit, they undergo a second trial, which consists of sup-

* 'Douze leçons sur l'Art de la Verrerie.'

porting for several weeks, and that without cracking or melting, a temperature far exceeding from 1800 to 2700 degrees Fahrenheit.

Each of these pots will last one or two, but rarely, three months.

CHAPTER III.

WINDOW GLASS.

HISTORICAL.

Does the use of glass as a means of preserving the interior of houses from the severity of the seasons go back to an indefinite period? or is it, as many persons think, a comparatively modern invention?

For a long time this question remained undetermined, for if on the one hand Winckelmann* pleaded the cause of antiquity, other scientific men, and by far the greater number, considered it a much more modern invention. This question, sustained as vehemently by the German archæologist as it was contested by his opponents, was in danger of for ever remaining in obscurity, when suddenly antiquity herself, tired doubtless of a discussion which threatened

---

* John Joachim Winckelmann, one of the most celebrated antiquaries of modern times, was the only son of a poor shoemaker of Steindalt (Brandenburg), and was born in that town on December 9th, 1717. He was assassinated at Trieste, on June 8th, 1768, by Francis Arcangeli, who suffered for his crime on the 20th of the same month. He left several remarkable works, amongst which we may mention the 'History of Art.'

her own honor, decided the question by proving that she had possessed window glass. And, indeed, the researches made at Pompeii have brought to light panes of glass which have remained fastened to their frames, although buried for more than seventeen hundred years under ashes.

To prevent a false idea being formed of the quality of Pompeian glass, we shall place before the reader the result of the chemical analysis made of it by M. Claudet, and also the formula now in use. From this comparison, if we bear in mind the continual advance of science, we shall see what state the glass of antiquity had attained.*

	Analysis of Pompeian glass, by M. Claudet.	Formula by M. Péligot, for window glass now used.
Silica	69·43	69·06
Lime	7·24	13·04
Soda	17·31	15·2
Alumina	3·55	1·8
Oxide of Iron	1·15	....
Oxide of Manganese	0·39	....
Copper	Traces	....
	99·07	99·1

It is scarcely possible to conceive that such a use-

---

* From what we have said of the Pompeian glass, it must not be concluded that, at that remote period, the windows of every house were glazed. The rarity of the window glass found in the ruins would rather tend to prove the contrary; but even considering the fact as very exceptional to the general custom, it is not the less proved that the ancients knew how to make window glass.

ful application of glass, which introduces light into our dwellings, and whilst allowing the regenerating rays of the sun to enter fiercely, and also protecting us from the frosts of winter, lengthens our life by doubling the duration of the day, should ever have been forgotten. And yet such was the case, for window glass disappeared entirely for several centuries, during which time it was replaced by wooden shutters, by semi-transparent stones, by skins, and lastly by oiled paper.

To find the first mention of glass being used to close, not dwelling-houses, but merely the narrow windows of churches, we must go back to the fourth century; for the most ancient author who mentions them is Lactantius,* who says: ". . . that our soul sees and distinguishes objects by the eyes of the body as through windows filled with glass." And yet we must not imagine that they were panes of glass such as we now know; for those of which this writer speaks were only small round pieces possessing little transparency, which were termed *cives*. As for dwelling-houses, the use of windows formed by a collection of small pieces of glass fastened together by lead does not go back further than the fourteenth century, and even then it was so rare that the windows of palaces were not all provided with them.

In the accounts of Jean Avin, receiver-general of Auvergne, we read :—

* Lactantius, born in Africa in the middle of the third century, died at Treves, 325 A.D.

"In preparation for Madame la Duchesse de Berry going (1413) to Montpensier, to have certain frames made for the windows of the said castle, to have them filled with oiled linen in default of glass."

Another example may be taken from the brilliant and luxurious court of the powerful dukes of Burgundy, for whose palace there were commanded (1467) "twenty pieces of wood to make frames for paper, serving as chamber windows."

These two quotations show the absence of glass even in the dwellings of princes, and we can now show the reader their rarity and the value still attached to them a century later.

In the document dated 1567, drawn up by the steward of the duke of Northumberland, we find the following:—

"And because during high winds the glass in this and the other castles of his lordship are destroyed, it would be well for the glass in every window to be taken out and put in safety when his grace leaves. And if at any time his grace or others should live at any of the said places, they can be put in again without much expense; whilst as it is at present, the destruction would be very costly, and would demand great repairs."

As a last proof of how recent is the general use of glass, it will suffice to say that at the close of the eighteenth century, not a hundred years ago, there existed, not only in provincial towns, but also in Paris itself, a corporation of makers of window-sashes, whose trade was to fill windows, not with glass, but merely with pieces of oiled paper. From this doubtless arose the old French proverb, "The abbey is poor, the windows are only of paper."

Now that we have become acquainted with the antiquity of glass, the different materials of which it is composed, the construction of the melting furnaces, the use of the pots, and have also learnt the meaning of such terms as frit, annealing, and fusion, which are the three principal operations in the glass-maker's art, we have only to occupy ourselves with the manufacture itself.

MANUFACTURE OF PLAIN OR FLUTED WINDOW GLASS.

Window glass may be manufactured by two very different processes, one of which produces what is termed crown glass, the other cylinder glass.

As the former process has not been employed in France for a long time, we shall only speak of the second.*

Before passing on, however, we think it better to rectify an erroneous opinion, very generally received, which attributes to Hugh Drolenvaux, superintendent of roads and bridges in Alsace, the first introduction into France of this method of blowing glass. It will be sufficient to compare the process given by the monk Theophilus (thirteenth century), in his "Essay

---

* Flint glass and crown glass being now especially used in the fabrication of optical glasses, we refer the reader to that article.

on diverse arts," with what we shall say of that now in use, to recognize that Hugh Drolenvaux only revived a method which had fallen into disuse.

We quote the words of the monk Theophilus (Book II. Chap. 6):—

"At the first hour in the morning, take an iron pipe, and if you wish to make sheets of glass, plunge the extremity of this pipe into a pot filled with glass. Turn the pipe in your hand until as much glass as you wish is collected round it, then taking it out, put it to your mouth and blow a little; removing it immediately, you put it to your cheek, so as not to draw the flame into your mouth when taking breath. Keep a smooth stone also before the window (of the furnace), on which you can beat the hot glass a little, in order to give it the same thickness all over; you must alternately blow and remove the pipe with great rapidity. When it presents the form of a long hanging bladder, bring the extremity of it to the flame, the glass soon melts, and you perceive an opening. Taking a wooden tool destined for this use, give the opening the size of the centre of the glass. Afterwards join the edges together, that is to say, the upper and lower sides, in such a manner that there may be an opening on each side of the junction. Immediately touch the glass near the tube with a damp wooden instrument, shake it a little, and it will be detached. Heat the pipe in the flame of the furnace until the glass which is on it becomes liquefied; place it quickly on the edges of the glass which you have united, and it will adhere; take it at once and expose it to the flame of the furnace until the glass around the opening from which you have taken the pipe becomes liquid. With a round piece of wood you must dilate this opening like the preceding one; and by bringing together the edges in the middle, and separating the pipe with the damp wooden tool, give it to an assistant, who, introducing some wood into the opening, will carry it to the annealing oven, which should be moderately heated. The kind of glass thus made is pure and white."

According to M. Péligot, ordinary window glass is composed of,

Silica	69·06
Lime	13·04
Soda	15·2
Alumina	1·8
	99·1

These different substances having undergone a first fusion by means of the frit, are poured into pots placed in the centre of the furnace, where they remain until they are perfectly melted, and have attained a pasty consistency, which is produced by the gradual lowering of the fire.

Then the workman and his assistant begin their labors, which we shall endeavor to make the reader understand by placing before him the different transformations that glass must undergo, from the moment in which the assistant, armed with his pipe, takes the first glass from the pot, until the sheet of glass, entirely finished by the blower, is ready for use.

Sheet glass, made from cylinders obtained by blowing, being employed for a number of objects in glass, we shall call our reader's special attention to this chapter, to which, however, we shall take care to refer him whenever necessary.

Before each glass pot two men are placed, the workman and his assistant.

The functions of the assistant, who has to do the rough part of the work, are to gather from the melting-pot with his pipe a certain quantity of the melting matter; to turn and return it on a small table of either marble or iron (see Fig. 19, page 129); to make it round by a slow and circular movement; then, lastly, to heat it again at the opening of the furnace.

When these four operations are terminated, the part of the assistant ceases, and that of the workman begins.

It is in these terms that M. Péligot describes the work of the glass-maker:—

"The workman at first blows lightly, drawing out the vitreous mass a little, so as to give it the form of a pear (Fig. 12, No. 1); he balances his cane (No. 2), then raises it so as to gather the glass (No. 3); he afterwards blows harder at short intervals, and gives it a movement backwards and forwards like the clapper of a bell, so as to lengthen the pear, which assumes a cylindrical form; he raises it rapidly over his head, then gives it a complete and rapid rotatory movement, in order to lengthen it (No. 4), whilst giving it an equal thickness in every part.

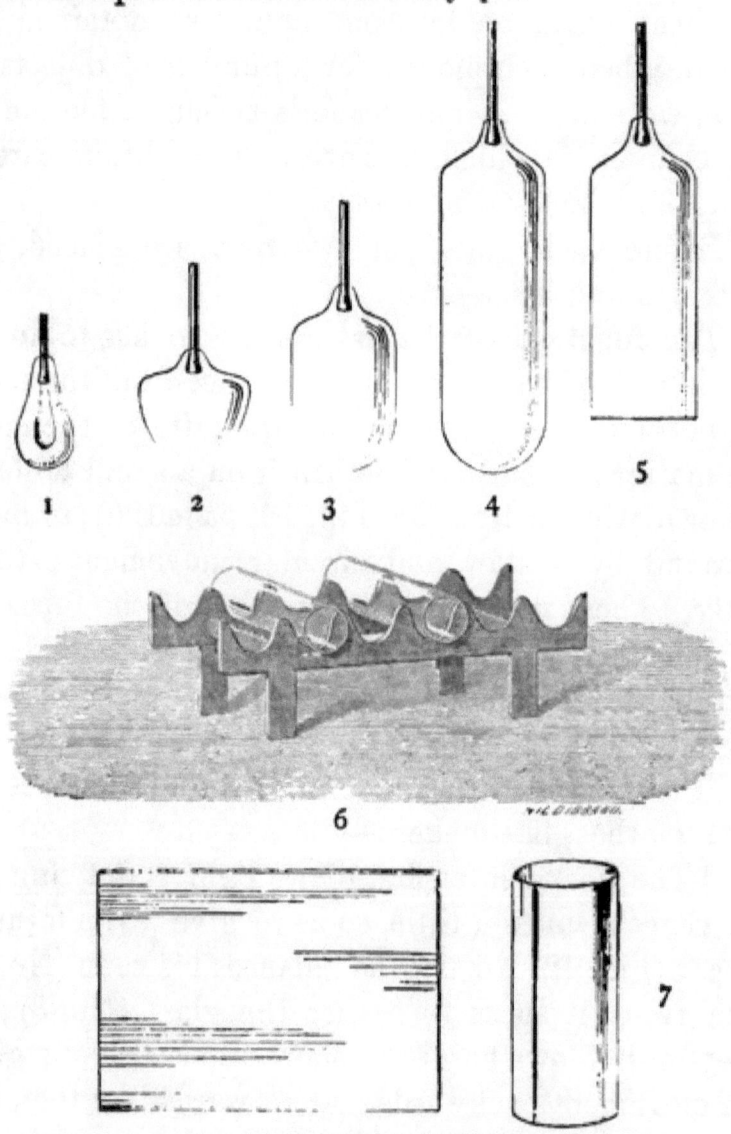

Fig. 12.—Blowing of Sheet Glass.

"When the cylinder is made, the blower brings it back to the opening of the furnace so as to soften the end; when it is sufficiently hot, it is pierced with an iron point. By the balancing movement the opening is increased; the glass is pared with a sort of wooden plate; the edges separate, and the top of the cylinder has disappeared (No. 5).

"When the cylinder has become firm, it is placed on a wooden rest (No. 6). The end of the pipe is touched with a cold iron rod; it separates immediately from the cylinder, which has already lost its bullion point, when a thread of hot glass is wound round it, and the part thus heated is touched with a cold iron rod. Thus we have now on the rest a cylinder open at each end. It is opened (No. 7) by passing a red hot iron rod down the interior in a straight line; one of the heated extremities being wetted with the finger, the glass bursts open. The same result may be attained by using a diamond attached to a long handle, which is passed down the interior of the cylinder by the side of a wooden ruler. This method, which is followed in Belgium, gives a straighter cut, and consequently involves less loss."

A perfectly plane surface has to be obtained from these split cylinders. To do this, they are taken to an oven which is heated to a dark red, and is termed the flattening oven. Here every cylinder is placed either on a sheet of thick glass, or on a slab of refractory earth, which has been previously powdered with gypsum or sulphate of antimony, in order to prevent the glass adhering to it. A workman, assisting the natural effect of heat, which tends to flatten the cylinders, makes a first gentle pressure on them with a long wooden pole; afterwards a wooden plane is passed over them, and lastly the *polissoir*, a wooden instrument which, moved lightly over the surface, makes it perfectly plane.

All the cylinders having become sheets of glass, the oven is hermetically closed; they remain in it several days, until they are sufficiently annealed and ready for use.

We must add that a rather recent discovery (1824), due to M. Robinet, a glass-blower in the manufactory at Baccarat, has founded a new era in the fabrication of all objects obtained by blowing.

The cylinders being produced as we have just seen by the breath of the workman, the objects blown can only attain a size proportionate to human strength, which is naturally very limited. Struck by this inconvenience, as well as affected by the effects of this labor, which not only exhausted young men, but also deprived those workmen who were weakened with age of all means of gaining a livelihood, M. Robinet substituted an implement for a workman by inventing a pump, by which cylinders of large dimensions may be manufactured.

M. Péligot describes it in these terms: " It is a small brass cylinder, closed at one end, in the interior of which there is an iron spring; in the lower part is a sort of wooden piston, with an opening covered with leather, retained in its place by a bayonet fastening pierced with a hole. The mouth of the pipe.

which is held vertically, is brought into contact with the piston; the air contained in the cylinder is compressed by a rapid movement given to the spring, and then injected to the glass which is being made."

This invention, doubly valuable both to humanity and trade, is now known by the name of the *Robinet Pump*. It has procured for its inventor a gold medal, adjudged by the Société d'Encouragement, and a pension from the directors of Baccarat.

FLUTED WINDOW GLASS.

The composition and manufacture of fluted window glass are exactly the same as for ordinary glass. The only difference is that the cylinder, instead of being made in the air, is blown in a cylindrical mould of cast iron, fluted in the interior, which impresses on the glass these flutings, preserved afterwards through the operation of blowing. For flutings crossed in squares, a mould is used, formed of two parts, which are separated when the cylinder is withdrawn

CHAPTER IV.

MIRRORS AND LOOKING-GLASSES.

The use of mirrors, abstracting them from their material, and considering them merely as rendering, by reflection, the exact image presented to them, goes back to the commencement of the human species, if we are to believe Milton, as Eve was the first to use them.

"That day I oft remember, when from sleep
I first awaked, and found myself reposed
Under a shade on flowers, much wondering, where
And what I was, whence thither brought, and how.
Not distant far from thence, a murmuring sound
Of waters issued from a cave, and spread
Into a liquid plain, then stood unmoved,
Pure as the expanse of Heaven. I thither went,
With unexperienced thought, and laid me down
On the green bank, to look into the clear
Smooth lake, that to me seemed a second sky.
As I bent down to look, just opposite,
A shape within the watery gleam appeared,
Bending to look on me: I started back,
It started back; but pleased, I soon returned,
Pleased it returned as soon, with answering looks
Of sympathy and love. There I had fixed
Mine eyes till now, and pined with vain desire,

Had not a voice thus warned me: 'What thou seest,
What there thou seest, fair creature, is thyself;
With thee it came and goes.'"

If to the name of Eve we add that of the beautiful Narcissus, who drowned himself in his mirror for

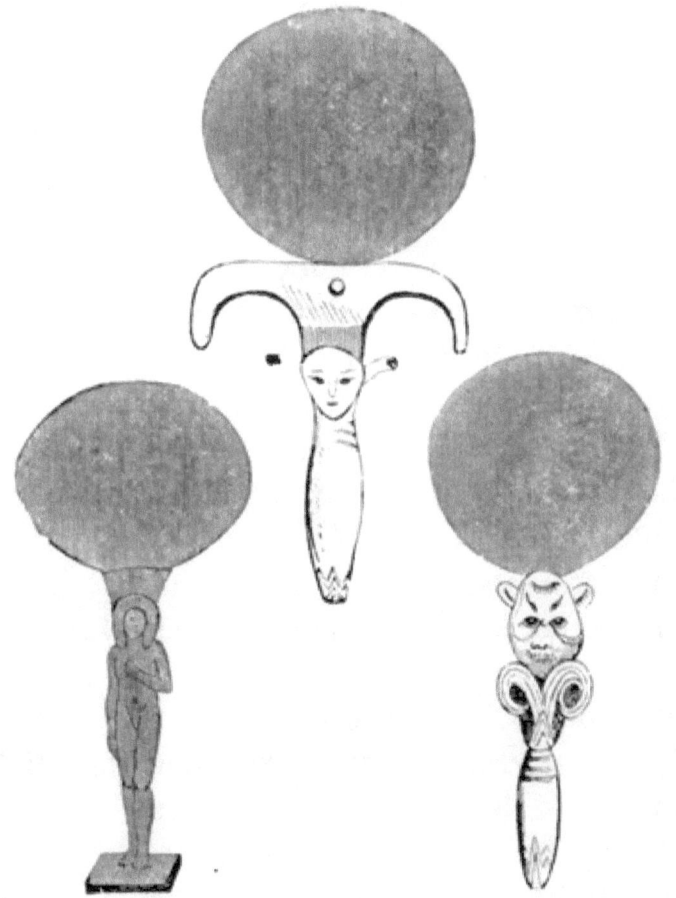

Fig. 13.—Egyptian Mirrors.

love of himself; and also that of Mahomet, who admired himself in a bucket of water, we shall no doubt have mentioned the three most illustrious partisans of the aquatic mirror.

As it was not always easy, even in those remote times, to have in one's own house a sheet of transparent water, it was replaced by something more portable, and there was then invented, at a time which cannot be known even approximately, the mirrors of polished metal which are first mentioned in the Old Testament. "Moses made the laver of brass, and the foot of it of brass, of the looking-glasses of the women assembling, which assembled at the door of the tabernacle of the congregation." (Exodus xxxviii. 8.)

Three types may be noticed in the form of the Egyptian mirrors, which passed from Egypt to Greece and Rome. According to Plutarch (Life of Numa Pompilius), "it was with a convex metal mirror that the Vestals relighted the sacred fire." Before attaining, however, to this degree of luxury, these mirrors must have passed through several rudimental stages both in form and style: indeed, the earliest metal mirrors, which have no ornaments whatever, are generally of the shape of an egg cut in half, the face of the cup alone being polished.

If these mirrors possessed the advantage of being more portable than those of Eve, Narcissus, and Mahomet, they had the inconvenience, not only of being of great weight, but also of deforming the features and even perhaps of making them look older. Such a crime was unpardonable; these enemies to beauty had to be replaced by others, and the mirrors of obsidian were substituted for them, which Pliny describes as a black stone, "sometimes transparent, but of such a dull transparency, that when used as a mirror it renders rather the shadow than the image of the objects."

Whilst fully granting that in the time of this author mirrors were made of metal, obsidian, or even of lapis specularis, must we blindly, and without venturing a criticism, adopt the opinion generally entertained, that glass mirrors are of modern invention, because the ancients did not know the process of plating, which alone can turn a piece of glass into a mirror?

The ancients are our masters in everything, whatever may be said to the contrary. Let us then endeavor to restore the honor of this invention to them who originated—however defective their knowledge of it may have been—the first idea of what modern industry assisted by science has now brought to such perfection.

As there are now no remains to be found, alas! of these ancient looking-glasses, we can only support our opinion by quotations from ancient writers, whose authority we hope will convince our readers of the antiquity of glass mirrors.

Pliny speaks of mirrors in several places. After those charming lines, "The discovery of mirrors belongs to those who first perceived their own image in the eyes of their fellow-men," he looks at the question from an historical point of view, and leaves no doubt as to the use of these mirrors; for, after having enumerated the different means employed in the fabrication of glass, which prove that in his time, and even before him, glass-makers "sometimes blew glass, sometimes fashioned it on the lathe, and sometimes carved it like silver," he adds: "Formerly Sidon was celebrated for its glass works; glass mirrors had even been invented there."

These words, *glass mirrors*, naturally implying the idea of glass reflecting an image, must we not necessarily allow that the ancients possessed a kind of plating which we do not know, and which, whether differing from our own or else identical with it, yet constituted a mirror?

The want of plating being the only point on which those authors rest who refuse the invention of looking-glasses to the ancients, let us see if we cannot find something in antiquity which disproves this assertion.

Aristotle, nearly four centuries before Pliny, is the first who alludes to the subject. He tells us: "If metals and stones are to be polished to serve as mirrors, glass and crystal have to be lined with a sheet of metal to give back the image presented to them."

And indeed, if a piece of colorless glass be placed on an opaque slab, even if it were only of black marble or slate, we have immediately a mirror, not indeed so limpid as those which decorate our drawing-rooms, but which will reproduce not merely the outline of the object, but also its different colors.

If to the words of Aristotle we add in thought

the certain improvements which the reflections of the philosopher have necessarily always suggested to the glass-makers of his time, we can no longer refuse to admit that a plating, or *lining* even, being shown to have been in use, glass mirrors, far from being, as is asserted, a modern invention, go back to a very remote period.

The fact of the antiquity of glass mirrors being thus established, as we are unable to follow the successive improvements in the manufacture, we will pass at once to the fourteenth century, to Venice, which, enjoying for centuries the exclusive and universal monopoly of glass-making, forms naturally a link to unite antiquity to modern times.

According to Lazari * it was only in the fourteenth century that the Venetians, following the advice of Aristotle, conceived the idea of replacing mirrors of polished metal by mirrors of glass, at the back of which they placed a metallic sheet.

The idea, or rather we should say its renovation, was progressive, and yet, whether it was that routine was against it, or that the result did not come up immediately to what was expected, it was abandoned, and metal mirrors became more fashionable than ever. They continued to be used until the two Muranezians, Andrea and Domenico d'Anzolo dal Gallo, who knew, or who had perhaps discovered for themselves, the method of manufacture already followed in Germany

* 'Notizia delle opere d'arte et d'antichità della raccolta Correr. Venezia, 1859.

and Flanders, addressed (1507) to the Council of Ten a petition, in which they said, "that, possessing the secret of making good and perfect mirrors of crystalline glass, a precious and singular thing unknown to the whole world, except to one glass manufactory in Germany, which, associated with a Flemish house, enjoyed the monopoly of this manufacture, and sold its productions in the East and West at excessive prices; and desiring to place Murano in a position to establish a competition which could not but be very profitable to the Republic, they demanded that an exclusive privilege should be granted to them in all the territory of the Republic during twenty-five years."

As this privilege promised to be profitable to the Republic, and possibly to assure her the means to monopolise another of the productions of glass-making, it was granted for twenty years.

The success of this enterprise surpassed all the hopes that had been entertained; consequently, the twenty years of privilege had scarcely expired, than there was a perfect rush of persons to embrace this new career. The number of mirror-makers became so great that in 1564 the Republic was obliged to separate them from the other glass-makers, and to establish a separate company for them.

As we have not space to mention here all those who improved the manufacture, we must be content with naming Liberale Motta, who about 1680, according to Lazari, "perfected it, and made mirrors of a size that until then had been unattainable."

Before passing on, it will be better to answer a question which has often been asked us: "Why are the mirrors of the fifteenth and sixteenth centuries, whether manufactured at Venice, Nuremburg, or in France, always of small dimensions?"

If our readers will kindly recall what has been said about window glass, which, blown by man, can never surpass a very limited size, they will have our reply, for window glass and mirrors were long obtained by the same process. It was reserved, as we shall soon see, for French modern industry to invent a new method of manufacture, which, known under the name of *founding*, can alone produce glasses of an almost unlimited size.

As we shall have to await the latter part of the sixteenth century to speak of French mirrors (until that time entirely neglected by fashion, which would have nothing but Venetian mirrors), let us see if this general infatuation was deserved.

Although fashion, that tyrannical queen of the world, scarcely ever takes reason as a companion, we must allow, were it only for the rarity of the fact, that this time she was right.

And indeed, could anything have come out from the hands of those Italians of the fifteenth century, who all of them artists, were then inventing, so to speak, the style of the Renaissance, which was at once so rich and so graceful, that did not bear the impress of that privileged period? As gold, silver, iron, wood, lead, everything, in short, was material for a masterpiece of some sort, it mattered little to them whether the mirror was large or small. In their eyes the frame was everything; it was that only which they could decorate, either with splendid carvings in wood, or with diamonds, rubies, or pearls.

Such costly frames necessarily appearing exaggerated in our century, when a frame more or less badly gilded is the *ne plus ultra* of elegance, we must refer those who would accuse us of exaggeration to the inventories of the dukes of Burgundy, of Louis of France, the duke of Anjou, Charles V., Margaret of Austria, etc., etc. There only will they be convinced of the distance that separates the pretended luxury of the present time, even in the highest classes, from what was in use in the palaces of the nobles in th fifteenth and sixteenth centuries.

Unhappily, of all this royal and princely magnificence there now only remains a cold dry mention. As for the objects themselves, the crucibles of the gold merchant can alone tell you how many have been destroyed in the last two centuries.

Notwithstanding the numbers destroyed during this artistic raid, brought on by cupidity on the one side, and kept up on the other by continual changes of fashion, several specimens have come down to us, though they are very rare, and one of these will show our readers what luxury was at the beginning of the seventeenth century.

We mean the mirror of the Queen Marie de Medici, exhibited in the *Musée des Souverains* at the

Louvre. The description we give of it, taken from the catalogue of that museum, will be heightened by the valuation made of it in 1791, which is contained in the inventory of the crown diamonds, printed in 1791, by order of the National Assembly (Fig. 14).

No. 102 in the catalogue. "It is of rock crystal, and agates, cut, polished, and set in a network of enamelled gold, form a frame around the glass which marks its rectangular form.

"This inner frame is surrounded by a larger one, every part of which is formed of precious stones; the fronton is of sardonyx, the two columns supporting it of oriental jasper; the base is highly decorated with camels cut in relief, and the pedestals of the columns which stand out over this base, the outlines of which they continue, are covered with slabs of sardonyx. Precious stones of the finest water glitter in the more conspicuous places on the frame, particularly three large emeralds; one of these, placed in the centre of the fronton, is set in the delicate details of a gold mounting, enriched with diamonds and rubies; the two others, placed on the side pedestals of the base, support helmeted heads or small busts, representing a warrior and an amazon. The face and neck are cut in the gem resembling a garnet, which jewellers call hyacinth; the helmets and the drapery which surrounds the breast are of enamelled gold, enriched with diamonds. Emeralds of smaller proportions, closely pressed against each other, serve as a setting for two carved stones; one of them, which is at the

Fig. 14.—Mirror of Marie de Medici (Louvre).

top of the whole construction, is an onyx of three layers, of antique carving; it is the head of a victory, winged and with a crown of laurel in her hair; the other stone is an onyx agate, with three layers, carved at the end of the sixteenth century; it is a female head in profile, draped, having a veil which falls from the head on to the shoulder, and wearing on her forehead the crescent of Diana. They are also emeralds which in threes decorate the frieze of the entablature, alternating with twelve small finely draped heads cut in hard stone of the fifteenth century, and which are portraits of the Cæsars."

The valuation made of this in 1791, was fixed at a hundred and fifty thousand francs (6000*l*., or $30,000 gold).

A hundred and fifty thousand francs being about its intrinsic and venal value, let there be added its artistic value, that derived from its history, its rarity, and above all the passion for collecting in our own days the rich spoils of that time, and we leave the reader to determine for himself what would now be the enormous price of such an object.

After such an artistic article of luxury, perhaps unique in Europe, we must leave the palace of the king to enter the country house of a rich burgess of the sixteenth century.

This word burgess, dear readers, need not alarm you even when we are speaking of art; for we must not forget that talent, at that time stamping indiscriminately every object in use, from the greatest to the smallest, whether it belonged to the suzerain lord or to the burgess; each one of them, being a product of the inspiration of the time, became by that fact alone an original work, unique and almost always remarkable.

To be convinced of the truth of our words, and to appreciate how much we, in the nineteenth century, owe to the ancient burgesses, it is only necessary to glance at these innumerable objects which, although destitute of crowns and emblazonment, do not the less form the glory and wealth of our museums.

Let us then leave, before the mirror of Marie de Medici, that group of spectators who, fascinated as they appear to be, yet do not dare to say what they most admire in it, whether the talent of the goldsmith or the enormous sum it now represents (the mere doubt says sufficiently clearly what any of them would do with it if he became its proprietor), and let us enter the burgess's house.

Here we find no diamonds or precious stones, but wood, ivory, iron, and tin; so if any lovers of the material have slipped in amongst us, let them lay aside their scales. Those who are fervent disciples of the balance and touchstone, as nothing here has any value but the ideal, solely due to the talent of the artist, must now make way for true lovers of art, who admire and esteem an object without troubling themselves whether it is of gold or copper. For those who love art before everything else, the intrinsic

Fig. 15.—Italian Mirror, with a Frame of Carved Wood (Louvre)

value of the material is and ever will be a secondary question, to be treated as worth so much the carat.

Now that "the sellers are driven out of the temple," let us gently take down this Italian mirror of the sixteenth century. Everything about it marks its great age; not only does it still bear the solid coarse iron ring by which it was fastened to the wall, but it has also preserved its primitive metallic slab, which confirms us in the opinion that, even posterior to the invention of glass mirrors, those of metal, less fragile and consequently easier of transportation, were still in use.

We must now return to the burgess's mirror, and see of what it is composed. (Fig. 15.)

It is a sheet of polished metal in a frame of carved wood.

Nothing could be more simple or primitive than this, or more dissimilar from the sumptuous mirror of Marie de Medici. And yet, notwithstanding its poverty, we do not hesitate to place it, if not in comparison with, yet at all events beside the royal mirror; for if the one possesses greater riches of material, the other possesses as indubitably all that the genius of man can give to what he touches; and it is because of this that we offer it to the reader as one of the most precious specimens of the glorious period of Italian Renaissance.

Although we are longing to come down to a more recent time, we must, unless we would be accused of making omissions, say one word about three other different kinds of mirrors, two of which especially have played an important part both as objects of fashion and of art. We mean:

> Des conseillers muets dont se servent les dames,
> Miroirs dans les logis, miroirs chez les marchands,
> Miroirs aux poches des galants,
> Miroirs aux ceintures des femmes,

which La Fontaine speaks of in his fable of " L'Homme et son image."

These portable mirrors were of two different shapes: some with handles, others almost round and of small dimensions.

We shall say little of the shape of those hand mirrors which the women wore at their girdles, for it would be to repeat almost word for word what we have said on Egyptian mirrors (page 89), the former being so to speak only a revival of the latter.

And indeed both of them, nearly always of metal polished and engraved, only differed in the system of ornamentation suitable to the different periods. In Egypt the style was severe; in France it is inspired by the Gallic spirit of the sixteenth century, not merely in offering subjects often rather free, but still more in the legends accompanying them. As there are exceptions to everything, we shall mention one which presents none of these inconveniences.

This Venetian mirror (sixteenth century), which is only four inches high and two wide, of embossed metal, gold and silver, is in the form of an X. On one side there is a metal mirror, on the other, a Love with bandaged eyes holding a bow.

The figure of the malicious god (old style) is surrounded by a legend, not new indeed, but too often true: AMOR DVCITVR EX OCVLI LVMINE CECVS (*Blind Love is led by the Light of the Eye*).

Fig. 16.—Ivory Box containing a Mirror.—Interior.

Small round glasses, whether of metal or glass, were enclosed in a round box, usually of ivory, opening into two equal parts, and which we cannot compare better than to the round tobacco boxes used by our fathers (Fig. 16). The mirror inside being o no interest to us, we will only occupy ourselves with the box containing it, for it possesses all the artistic interest.

Many collections possess separate parts, sometimes an upper and sometimes a lower half; but a complete whole mirror is so difficult to find, that during a thirty years' search, the indefatigable Sauvageot, a man who sacrificed everything to complete his collection, could find but one, which we place before the reader.

If the costumes of the figures were not sufficient to fix the date of this mirror in the middle of the fifteenth century, the subjects represented on the two valves would do so. One of them represents the attack on the Castle of Love, and the other a lance combat of two knights at the foot of a tower (Fig. 17).

Both subjects are doubtless taken from some romance of chivalry then fashionable.

SILVERED LOOKING-GLASSES, WITH A FRAME OF EITHER SILVERED OR COLORED GLASS.

We must now say a few words about those Venetian glasses which, after having been so long laid by in lumber-rooms, seem to be once more coming into fashion, thanks to the revival of artistic taste, which is leading the present generation to seek for and imitate the works of that period. We mean those looking-glasses, the frames of which are also composed of glass, either silvered like the mirror itself, or else colored.

Fig 17.—Ivory Box containing a Mirror.—Exterior.

As, owing to the scarcity of original looking-glasses of the sixteenth century, it is very difficult to make a comparison between them and those made in our own days, we consider it necessary to show the reader a glass (Fig. 18) which certainly from its destination must have been considered perfect: it is that in the Cluny Museum, which, it is said, was offered by the Republic of Venice to Henry III., on his return from Poland.

It is only after having compared it with those of the present day that we can form a just idea of the numerous improvements successively introduced into the manufacture of looking-glasses; for if it possesses the merit of being perhaps the largest that could have been obtained by blowing, it must be acknowledged that it leaves much to be desired in respect of purity, covered as it is with air-bubbles and striæ. For the honor of the Venetian glass-makers, we must add that these defects, almost unknown at the present time, were inevitable in the method of blowing then in use.

The frame of colored and white glass bevelled, is decorated with fleurs-de-lis and palm leaves alternately. Each of them is fixed on the frame by a screw with a head.

Now that we have mentioned the principal forms of mirrors, and have given the reason for their small size, let us pass to Paris, and see by what means France succeeded, after many fruitless efforts, in freeing herself from the tribute rendered to Venice, which town, supported by fashion, had enjoyed the monopoly in mirrors.

The fashion for looking-glasses was so great, that in his virelay on *l'excès où l'on porte toute chose* (the excess to which everything is carried), Regnier Des marets tells us:

> " Dans leurs cabinets enchantés
> L'étoffe ne trouve plus place;
> Tous les murs des quatre cotés
> En sont de glaces incrustés.
> Chaque coté n'est qu'une glace.
> Pour voir partout leur bonne grâce,
> Partout elles (les femmes) veulent avoir
> La perspective d'un miroir."

This luxury, however, was only a fashion renewed from the Romans. Seneca (Epis. 86) informs us that, in his time, "the man esteemed himself very poor who had not his room surrounded with sheets of glass."

Being no longer able to tolerate a tribute, as humiliating for the mirror-makers as ruinous for the country (the importation was estimated at more than a hundred thousand crowns a-year, an enormous sum for that time), Louis XIV., or rather Colbert, recurred to the ideas of Henry II. (1551), of Henry IV., and of Louis XIII. (1634), and resolved to give a mortal blow to the importation, by founding at Paris a large manufactory of looking-glasses in the Venetian style.

To attain this result, they had to obtain from the

Fig. 18.—Mirror of Henri III. (Cluny Museum.)

very prudent and very suspicious Republic the secret which she preserved with so much care relative to all the operations of glass-making.

Two means only could succeed—force and cunning.

Colbert, preferring the second means, wrote (1664) to François de Bonzi, bishop of Béziers, at that time French ambassador to the Republic of Venice, not only to obtain the secret of the manufacture, but also secretly to hire Venetian workmen for France.

This order, which was very easy to give from Versailles, was, as we shall see, much more difficult to execute at Venice. The ambassador, after having doubtless sounded his way, replied, a short time after, that to send workmen to France, he ran the risk of being thrown into the sea.

Such a danger threatening an ambassador of the court of France, would perhaps have dissuaded any other minister; but either considering the fears of the bishop chimerical, or else recognizing them as real, but without danger to himself, Colbert, who certainly thought more of his own idea than of the life of Bonzi, again ordered him not to lose sight of the instructions he had previously given him.

As Colbert had no doubt thought, the fear of displeasing him was more powerful than that of being thrown into the sea, and a short time after (1665) by force of address, money, and promises, eighteen Venetian workmen, flying from their country, arrived at Paris.

These eighteen Venetian glass-makers were sufficient to found a glass factory. Colbert at once organized a company which, placed under the orders of Nicolas du Noyer, receiver-general at Orleans, opened an establishment (1665) in the Faubourg St. Antoine, on the site now occupied by the barracks of Reuilly, under the title of *Manufactory of Glass Mirrors by Venetian Workmen.*

Like the commencement of every great industry, that which we speak of, although patronized by an all-powerful minister, had to undergo rude shocks from the discontent of the Venetian workmen, who accused the court of France of not keeping the promises that had been made to them.

Whether or no this reproach was well founded, it is none the less true that disorder soon crept into the establishment, less perhaps through the furtive departure of several of the Venetians, than by the ill-feeling of those who, engaged to teach pupils, only appeared to remain in order to hinder the works intrusted to them.

Colbert's great idea was then in peril, when a chance, as fortunate as it was unexpected, came to his assistance. In the year 1673 the minister found himself in a position to reply to M. de Saint-André, ambassador at Venice, who offered him mirror-makers from Murano: " The manufacture is sufficiently well established in the kingdom to have no need of them." And, indeed, France now sufficed for herself; the importation of Venetian mirrors had been prohibited since 1669.

These are the means by which the French succeeded in making looking-glasses notwithstanding the ill-will of the Venetians.

The manufacture in the Faubourg St. Antoine was about to extinguish its furnaces, when M. de Chamillart informed Colbert that there existed at Tourlaville, near Cherbourg, a manufactory of white glass and looking-glass in the Venetian fashion, which, directed by Richard Lucas, Sieur de Nehou, enjoyed a certain reputation.

How could a simple individual become master of a secret refused to the power of Colbert, and how was it that Colbert did not know of the existence of this manufactory?

Without undertaking to reply here to the second question, we come at once to the first.

According to the chronicle, several young men of Strasbourg, having left their native town in order to learn the art of glass-making, agreed to take a journey to Venice, hoping that after having served an apprenticeship in a mirror manufactory, they might bring back to France the knowledge and the practice they would have acquired in a foreign land. Their hopes were not however of long duration; few days had elapsed since their arrival at Murano, when each of them had been pitilessly refused by the glass-makers, for whom every foreigner was an enemy. Being then unable to learn openly, they had recourse to ruse; and this, according to the tradition, is the means they employed. Profiting by the moment when the Venetians, jealous even of each other, were working in all security at their looking-glasses, doors and windows closed, our young Strasbourgeois, perched on the roof, and watching their movements through skilfully-managed holes, succeeded after many dangers in learning the secrets, or rather the *tour de main* which alone constituted the supremacy of the glass-makers of Murano.

As skilful now as their masters, the young men returned to France and offered their services to Lucas de Nehou, who, as may be imagined, eagerly availed himself of them. It was thus that mirrors in imitation of the Venetian ones were introduced into France.

To turn the new importation to profit, Colbert annexed the glass-works of Tourlaville to the royal manufactory at Paris. Very soon, assisted by this intelligent minister, Lucas de Nehou freed, thanks to the title of royal manufactory, from many embarrassments which had paralysed his labors, and provided with greater privileges, advanced so steadily in his improvements, that it was from the glass-works of Tourlaville, directed by him, that the first fine French looking glasses came.

For a growing industry there are two kinds of protectors—one of them common enough, who says to you: You have obtained what you demanded, now the rest is your own business; the other much rarer, who not only enables you to produce, but who, by his social influence, attracts the public towards you.

Neither of these benefactors was wanting to Richard de Nehou; after having met with a Colbert he was fortunate enough to find a Louis XIV.

At this period, to have the sovereign in one's favor was to attract the court and the town; and this was what happened, for as soon as courtiers, rich contractors, and even burgesses learned that their king had not only had French looking-glasses put in his carriages (1672), but had even given the order at the royal manufactory for all those required to decorate the great gallery at Versailles (from which arose its name of the *gallerie des glaces*, which it still bears); each of them, eager to pay his court to the king and the minister, hastened, notwithstanding the high price at which looking-glasses then were, to flock to the royal manufactory.

An anecdote related by Saint Simon proves that flattery was not cheap.

"In 1699 the countess of Fiesque, who had been one of the marshals of the camp of Mademoiselle de Montpensier at the attack on Orleans, and who had scarcely anything left, because she had allowed everything to be wasted or stolen by her attendants, bought an extremely fine mirror, at a time when these magnificent glasses were still very rare and very costly. 'Well, countess,' said one of her friends, 'where did you get that?' 'I had,' replied she, 'a troublesome estate (une méchante terre), which only brought in corn. I have sold it, and bought this mirror with it. Have I not done wonders?'"

Thus encouraged by the court and the nobility the royal manufactory of looking-glasses doubtless conceived great hopes for the present. But was there nothing to be feared for the future? Venice still existed, and braving the severe penalties pronounced against all introduction of foreign glass into France, smuggling, certain of a sale, were it only from the critics at the court, went on actively, and did much harm to French industry.

In order to destroy this disastrous competition, two things were required: a lower price in the manufacture, which might enable them to sell cheaper than the Venetians, and more perfect work.

It may be remembered that it was Richard Lucas de Nehou, who died in 1675, that had first dared to raise the standard of independence against the Venetian monopoly. It was his son, Louis Lucas de Nehou, who gave it the last blow, first by inventing, in 1688, the method of founding glass, which, as we shall see, allows the manufacture of glasses of an almost unlimited size, and afterwards by removing the establishment from Paris to St. Gobain.

All that we have said on the manufactory of St. Gobain, which is certainly the most perfect example that we could give of everything that concerns the making of looking-glasses, having been in great part extracted from the excellent work of M. Auguste Cochin,* a member of the Institute, we ask the au-

---

* 'La Manufacture des Glaces de St. Gobain, de 1665 à 1865. Paris, Donniol, 1866, page 72.

thor's permission, in behalf of our readers, to complete this article by quoting his own words.

"The first improvement was the invention of founding. I believe that there does not exist in all the wo derful processes employed in manufacture, a more marvellous operation, or one that requires a greater mixture of strength, skill, courage, and rapidity.*

"When one enters for the first time into one of the vast glass-houses of St. Gobain at night, the furnaces are closed, and the dull sound of a violent though captive fire alone interrupts the silence. From time to time a workman opens the *working-hole* to look into the furnace at the state of the glass; long blueish flames then light up the sides of the annealing ovens, the blackened beams, the heavy flattening tables, and the mattresses in which half-naked workmen sleep quietly.

"Suddenly the hour strikes, the call is beaten on the iron slabs which surround the furnace, the whistle of the foreman is heard, and thirty strong men stand up. The manœuvres begin with the activity and precision of an artillery movement. The furnaces are opened, the glowing pots are seized and raised into the air by mechanical means; they pass like

---

* According to M. Péligot the St. Gobain glass is composed of,
Silica.................................... 73·0
Lime .... 15·5
Soda .... 11·5
                                          ─────
                                          100·0

hanging globes of fire along the beam, then stop, and are lowered over the immense cast-iron table, placed with its roller before the open mouth of the annealing oven. The signal given, the pot leans over, and the beautiful opal liquid, brilliant, transparent, and unctuous, falls and spreads over the table. At a second signal the roller passes over the red-hot glass; a workman, with his eyes fixed on the fiery substance, skims off the apparent defects with bold and skilful hand; then the roller falls or passes off, and twenty workmen provided with long shovels quickly push the glass into the oven, where it is annealed and cools slowly. The workmen then turn round and begin again, without disorder, without noise, without rest. The founding goes on for an hour, the pots are immediately refilled, the furnaces reclosed, darkness again falls, and the continuous noise of the fire preparing fresh work is again the only sound heard.

"When the glass has been placed in the annealing oven it remains there about three days.

"The process of taking it out is less dramatic than the casting. And yet it is striking to see twelve workmen, with no other help than leather bands, draw out, raise, and carry this large, thin, and fragile glass, walking in step like soldiers, from the annealing oven to the desk (*pupitre*), placed on wheels and rails, which will convey it still unpolished to the *squaring* room, where it will be examined, classified, cut, and sent to other workrooms to be finished.

"The glass is already beautiful, but opaque; it

has to become transparent, polished, and perfectly even. As it has to transmit or reflect light, no defect in it must disperse or obscure the rays. This fragile glass has then to be abraded with sand, imbedded in plaster of Paris, and *smoothed* with emery against another glass which is fixed; it has to be turned, to smooth the other side, and *soaped* with the hand, then polished by rubbing it with woollen cloth covered with red oxide of iron, all of which is done by means of complicated instruments set in movement by steam or water. Afterwards it has to be raised and examined a second time, and when it is perfect, sent to the room where it will be classed, silvered, or cut, and then sold."

According to the same author, the plating is done at St. Gobain in the following manner:—" On an inclined table surrounded by gutters, a carefully cleaned sheet of tin is spread, on which the mercury is poured. Under a light and rapid hand, the glass, pushed straight forward, drives before it the surplus of the metal, and the mercury, shut in between the tin and the glass, spreads out, adheres and amalgamates in a few minutes. But the glass has to dry for nearly eight days, under heavy weights, which completes the fixing of the tinfoil."

Besides the difficulty of beating and flattening the tin without tearing it, and the excessively high price of mercury, the method of plating we have just described, which is still generally followed, presents a far more serious inconvenience, for notwithstanding all imaginable precautions, it affects the health of the workmen in the greatest degree.

Wishing to remedy this danger, M. Petitjean invented, in 1855, a new process of plating, by means of tartaric acid, nitrate of silver, and ammonia. This process is beautiful to watch; two liquids as colorless as water are poured on the glass, and after a few moments the silver appears and spreads uniformly over the glass. Until now glasses silvered in this manner have presented the inconvenience of becoming covered with spots, but fresh attempts allow us to hope that they will be as fine as the quicksilvered glasses, and will be more largely used. It is said that a mirror is dangerous for any one who looks much in it; this is unhappily still more true for the workman who plates it; the new process will deserve at once the praises of manufacturers and of humanity in general.

We cannot better finish this chapter than by giving a list of the changes of price in looking-glasses, from 1699 to 1862.

In 1699 the countess of Fiesque gave a *mauvaise terre*, which brought in corn, for one mirror.

	£	s.	d	$ cts., in Gold.
In 1702 a yard of glass cost	6	12	0	32 11
In 1802 " "	8	4	0	39 90
In 1862 " "	1	16	0	8 76

This decrease in price is still more considerable,

according to M. Cochin, when we come to glass of larger dimensions.

	£	s.	d.	$ cts., in Gold.
In 1702 a glass of 4 yards was worth	110	0	0	535 32
In 1802* " "	145 15	0	709 30
In 1862 " "	10 10	0	51 09

* In 1802, after the revolution, and especially in 1805, during the continental blockade, the prices were higher than a century earlier.

CHAPTER V.

BOTTLES.

HISTORICAL.

Many persons still believe that the ancients, who rejoiced in so many kinds of luxury, were much less advanced in the ordinary objects of life. To believe them, we might almost suppose that the earthen or wooden bowl that Diogenes threw from him as too luxurious (or at all events as useless, since he could drink out of the hollow of his hand), was the goblet generally in use; and that, ignorant of the art of preserving wines, every guest at the table pressed the grapes into the cup with his own hands.

By a few quotations from their own writings, we will endeavor to show that the ancients, who gave a god to the vine, were too good pagans to preserve and drink the gifts of Bacchus in vases unworthy the majesty of the god.

Did the ancients employ bottles and drinking glasses?

To these two questions, which have been sometimes answered in the negative, we would unhesitatingly reply: Yes, the ancients did use them; for Egypt, that glorious old Egypt, has left us bottles made of simple glass, and others covered with wicker-work or papyrus stalks. The latter, which offer the greatest resemblance to those used for Florence oil, are still used by the Egyptians under the name of *damadjan*.

If we pass over many centuries, during which there is nothing to prove that the manufacture of bottles had ceased, and come down to the Romans, we shall there find the similarity still more striking; for, as we shall see, there are no longer merely glass vessels something like our own, but bottles identical with those we now employ.

Four lines from Horace and a few words of Petronius will prove this:—

"I wish to celebrate the anniversary, and this happy day will make the cork and the seal of an amphora fly that was put in the smoke under the consulate of Tullus."*

"They immediately bring glass bottles carefully *sealed;* on the neck of each is a *label,* marked thus: 'Opinian Falernian,† one hundred years old."‡

In these quotations, the number of which we

---

* 'Horace to Mæcenas,' ode vii., book iii., line 9.

† The name of Opinian Falernian was given to the Falernian wine made under the consulate of Opinius (year of Rome, 634). Pliny (book iv. chap. iii.) says that in his time some of this Falernian still existed. At that time it must have been about two hundred years in the bottle.

‡ Petronius, 'Satyricon,' book xxxiv.

could easily have increased,* do we not find the bottle, the cork, the wax that covers it, and even the label, to indicate the nature of the wine? In short, we find the bottle as it is now used.

From the antiquity of bottles must we conclude that they have been uninterruptedly in general use to the present day? If their utility might lead us to think so, the absence of any object of the kind, and the silence of authors on the subject, refute that opinion; for the two most ancient documents that we can quote are, first, one which mentions as the earliest glass bottle factory in France, that which existed at Quicangrogne (Aisne), in 1290; and another (the Rolls of the city of Paris) which (1292) speaks of some one named "Macy, qui fet des bouteilles" (who makes bottles).

If the former document leaves no doubt as to the sort of bottles, it is not the same with the latter. This Macy may have made bottles of other materials than glass, for we must not forget that in the thirteenth and fourteenth centuries the kings of France used indiscriminately, either bottles of enamelled silver or simple leathern bottles, which, imported from England, were afterwards imitated at Paris. It even appears that a certain Jehan Petit Fay, a "merchant following the court" (1469), was commissioned to supply the court of Louis XI. with them.

* Martial, 'Epigrams,' books XIII. cxx. "If the wine of Spoleto had been kept some years in the bottle, you would prefer it to new Falernian."

It was, then, only about the end of the fifteenth century, or even at the beginning of the sixteenth, that glass-works became so numerous in France as to replace leathern bottles by glass ones.

MANUFACTURE OF ORDINARY BOTTLES.

Silica, soda or potash, lime, alumina, and oxide of iron, are the constituent parts of glass bottles.

Although the blower and boy are sufficient for the manufacture of sheet glass, two more workmen are required for bottles.

The functions of the several workmen are as follows.

The gatherer takes some glass from the pot and passes the blowing iron thus laden to an assistant,

Fig. 19.—Manufacture of Bottles.—Preparation of the Glass.

who, after having added a fresh quantity of glass, gives it a rotatory movement, by which means the glass ball becomes lengthened. The blower then takes the pipe, places the glass ball in an earthen mould surrounded with iron bands, blows, and this mass, just now so shapeless, becomes a bottle.

The bottle is not yet finished however, for the bottom has to be completed, the neck to be decorated with the usual small glass band, and the bottle to be marked with the stamp indicating either the glass manufactory or the nature of the wine.

The first of these operations is performed by pressing the lower part of the bottle with a conical instrument as soon as it comes out of the mould; the second by winding a thick glass thread round the extremity of the neck; and the third by adding some fresh glass at the side of the bottle and stamping it with a seal.

The claret bottles having flat bottoms are blown by the Robinet pump, of which we have already spoken, in an iron mould with hinges, invented by M. Carillon. They are lighter than the usual bottles, and although they only weigh about one pound ten ounces, yet they contain nearly one pint and a quarter.

France manufactures annually from about 60,000 tons of bottles (each bottle weighing about two pounds three ounces), nearly 23,000 tons of which are for exportation. More than 10,000 tons are required for champagne alone.

Whilst fully admitting the great improvements made in the manufacture of bottles by the skill of modern workmen, we must mention three great de-

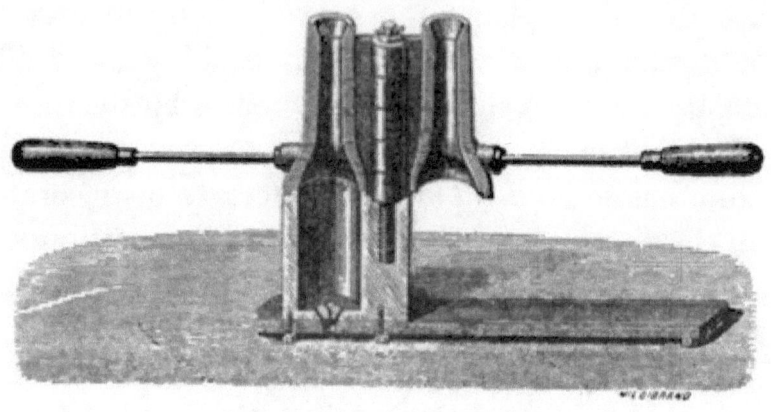

Fig. 20.—Mould for Claret Bottles.

fects, their opacity, their want of elegance, and invariable uniformity in shape. These defects, which doubtless were greater formerly than at the present time, induced the Italians of the sixteenth century, who sought elegance, color, form, and artistic work, to banish these sad-looking bottles from their gay feasts, and to replace them with splendid bottles of thin colorless glass, decorated, sometimes with a light gold lacing, sometimes with fine arabesques in colored enamel, through which the rich colors of their generous wines might be seen.

From our love, or rather our grateful veneration for the artists of past times, who, as true and intelligent pioneers, have prepared the way in all the arts and in every trade, it must not be thought that we are indifferent to the present state of manufacture or doubtful of its progress. We would only declare war against bad taste, against certain manufacturers who encourage it, and also against those lovers of antiquity who deny the progress.

We declare war then to the bad taste which so often prevails in all classes of society, which calls grace what is only affectation, richness of coloring what is only a monstrous assemblage of colors, and originality what is only singularity!

War also to the manufacturers who, shamelessly deserting the standard of art, debase themselves so far as to truckle to the bad taste of the public!

As for the exclusive admirers of antiquity, although the wrong done by them is of a totally different nature, for it is derived from whatever is most noble in our sentiments, the worship of memories, must they not be accused of conspiring against modern industrial art, not only by denying its progress, but also by constantly affirming its inferiority to past ages?

And this, too, at the present time, when artistic instruction is more widely spread than ever, when manual dexterity has attained an extraordinary degree of excellence, and when chemistry supplies materials far superior to those which were formerly used! No, we may honor the efforts of the ancients, and admire their works; we may recognize them as our masters; but let us not forget that notwithstanding the progress we owe to them, and the improvements made by the laborers who have succeeded each other for ages, we shall always have to work in the field of intelligence, for in the sciences, the arts and

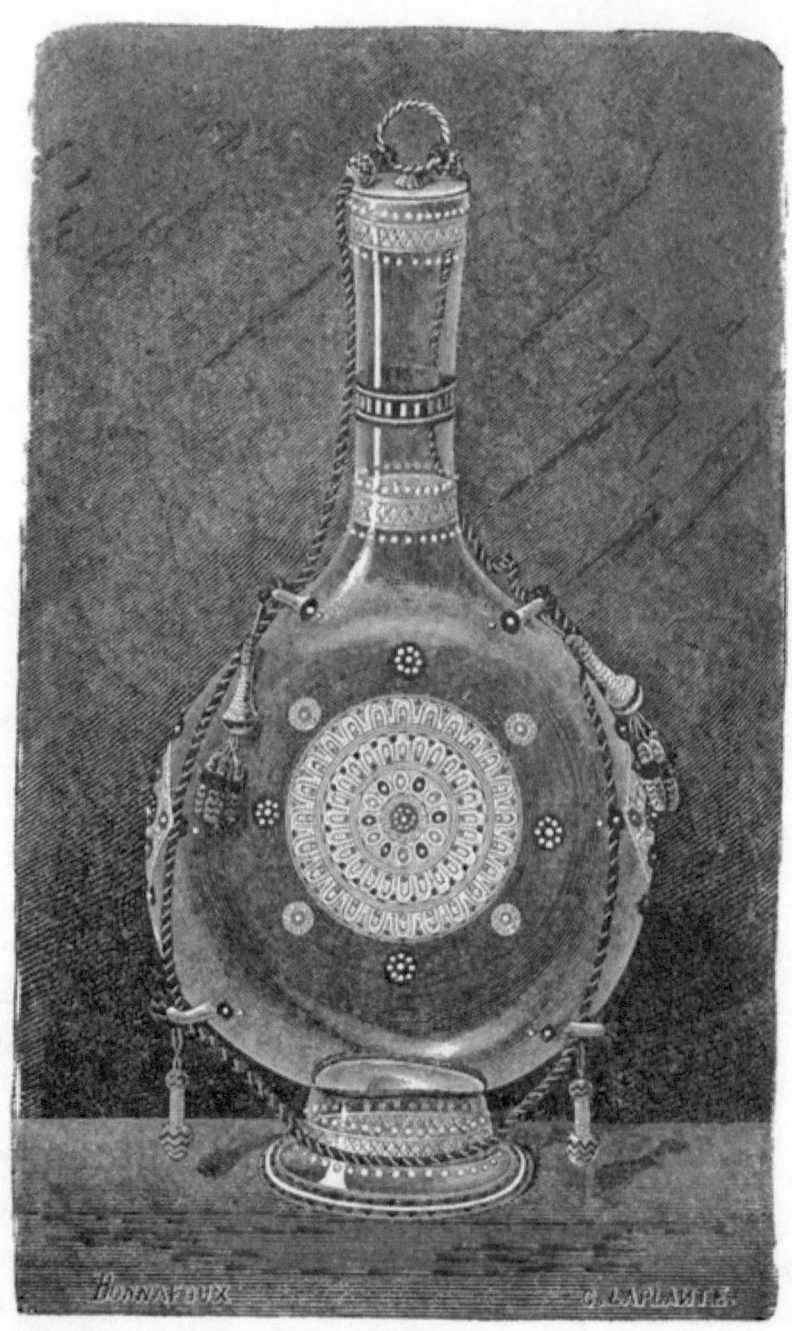

Fig. 21.—Venetian Bottle.

manufactures, the only goal that can be assigned is what man will never reach—perfection.

To prove that industrial art has not degenerated, we shall offer the reader a specimen of a glass jug which, certainly from its lightness, the elegance of its shape and its extreme limpidity, will, we hope, be a convincing proof that there still exists in France some manufacturers who make noble efforts to lead the public taste towards the beautiful.

This glass jug (Fig. 23) which certainly may bear comparison with any Italian production, was made at

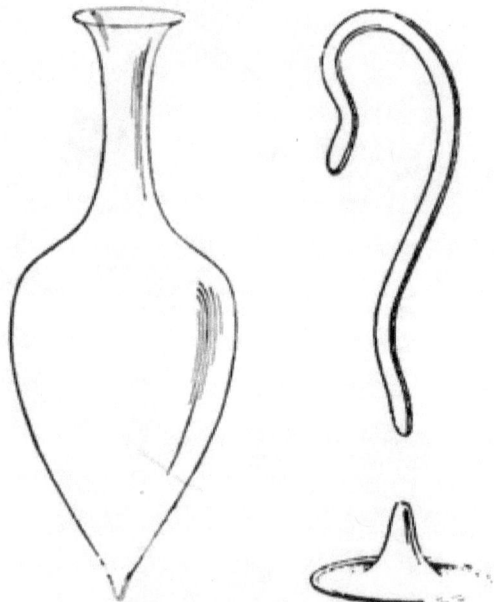

Fig. 22.—Construction of the Jug; Fig. 23.

the crystal works of Clichy-la-Garenne, in 1867, and it is not by any means a solitary example, as there are many others as remarkable, which we shall hope at a proper time to place before the reader.

As we have already described the method of making ordinary bottles, we shall now occupy ourselves with that used for vases, or bottles having a handle and foot, for we wish to confute an error generally received, that these vases are obtained at once by means of a mould; while, on the contrary, they require three manual operations, one corresponding to each of the distinct and very different parts forming the vase, the body, the foot, and the handle. It is by taking the vase to pieces that we shall prove it.

The design of the vase being given, the glassmaker takes from the pot with his pipe the amount of glass he considers necessary, and then marvers and blows it. As soon as the form (generally ovoid) is obtained, a second workman fastens to the lower part of the vase a piece of crystal which has been shaped by him to form the foot. The vase, which is still incomplete, having been again heated, repaired, and the neck widened and cut with the shears,* a third workman, who has prepared a tube of the shape desired, fastens it to the body and thus forms the handle, which completes the vase.

This is the method of making them, very different, as may be seen, from the generally received opinion.

* Glass in a malleable state may be cut very easily with ordinary shears.

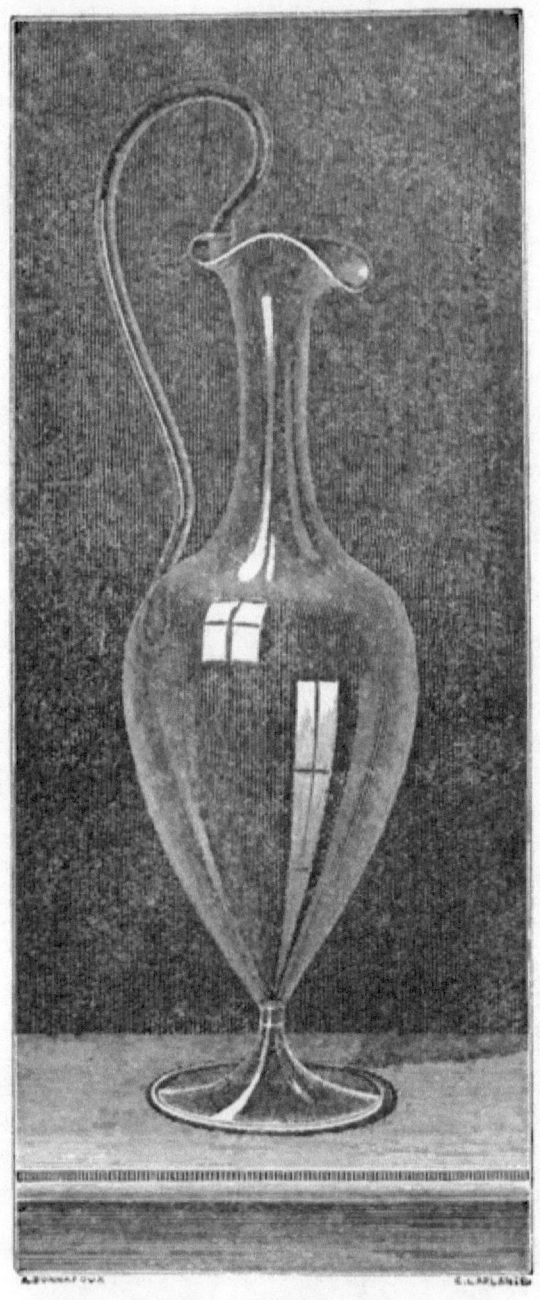

Fig. 23.—Jug (Glass Works of Clichy.)

CHAPTER VI.

GOBLETS AND DRINKING-GLASSES.

After bottles we come to goblets and drinking glasses, which, although they differ in form, name, and sometimes in material, especially those of olden time, are nevertheless all employed for the same purpose.

As, since the beginning of the world men must always have drunk, and as there have always been some who loved the luxuries of the table, it must be admitted, not only that the more refined did not drink out of the bottle, but also that Diogenes,* who threw away his bowl (thinking it more convenient to drink out of the hollow of his hand), did not found a school.

The probable use of goblets and glasses being admitted, let us endeavor to confirm it from history. Solomon (Proverbs xxiii. 29, 30, 31) is the first writer whose authority we shall quote. "Who hath redness of eyes? They that tarry long at the wine; they that go to seek mixed wine. Look not thou upon the wine when it is red, when it giveth his color in the cup."

* Diogenes, born at Sinope (Asia), 413 b.c.

Since the time of the wise man who lived a thousand years before Christ, glass cups have been in use, for we find them used in marriage ceremonies amongst the ancient Hebrews. The high priest presented to the husband and wife a cup filled with wine, which, after they had both sipped from it, was broken to atoms.*

Having only to occupy ourselves with glass, we must, for fear of going beyond the limits marked out for us, leave on one side the gold and crystal goblets —which from the Homeric ages had been used either in sacrifices or in feasts—in order to mention as briefly as possible the struggle which glass had to sustain against these two rivals—rivals the more dangerous as the richness of the material at that time, as well as in our own, was, and always will be of great importance in the estimation of mankind. Consequently the struggle was long and stubborn, for if the cause of the gold and crystal goblets was energetically sustained by the partisans of ancient customs, other enthusiasts, less conservative, sang the praises of the more recent invention.

The triumph of glass appeared certain, when suddenly confusion entered the camp of the progressionists. Some wished that the purple glass cups, which were made at Diospolis and Alexandria, should be

* This ceremony, which is still practised, is a symbol of the fragility of human nature, which Isaiah describes as follows: "The grass withereth, the flower fadeth, but the word of our God shall stand for ever."

exclusively adopted, whilst others voted for those of which Vopiscus speaks in the Life of Saturninus, and which were made in Egypt in various colors.

Neither party being willing to make the least concession, the cause of the glass cups would have been perhaps lost for ever, or at least for an indefinite period, when a third party, profiting by the confusion, proclaimed the introduction of transparent glass. Such are in fact the words of Pliny when he says, speaking of glass (Book xxxvii. Chap. 67), "No material is more easily handled, or takes colors better; but the most esteemed is colorless and transparent glass, because it more resembles crystal. It has even superseded metal drinking cups."

Transparent glass having thus gained the day, let us remain at Rome, whither we have been brought by Pliny, for we shall find there one of the most ancient specimens, not of cups but of drinking glasses. Let the reader refer back to Fig. 6, on page 29, and he will see that the ancient Romans, whilst perhaps using only cups, had however also some kinds of glasses very similar to ours. If this specimen be not sufficient, we can quote three lines of Horace (Satire IV. Book ii.), which will not leave any doubt; for he says,

> "Magna movet stomacho fastidia, seu puer unctis
> Tractavit calicem manibus, dum furta ligurrit,
> Sive gravis veteri crateræ limus adhæsit."

The lines, moreover, with which Boileau is inspired

when he says, in his description of a ridiculous repast,

*   *   *   *   *   *

"On a porté partout des verres à la ronde
Où les doigts des laquais, dans la crasse tracés
Témoignoient par écrit qu'on les avoit rincés."

The use of drinking glasses, which the Romans doubtless received from a more ancient nation, soon spread throughout Europe, and to such a degree that glass-works became very numerous.

Not being able to follow here step by step the successive periods of the establishment of even the principal centres of glass manufacture, for this would carry us much too far, we must content ourselves with pointing out the principal difference which exists among them in the quality of the glass, in the shape, and the most usual style of ornament.

GERMAN GLASS.

German glasses, of a greenish or yellowish color are generally of a cylindrical shape. An enamelled painting is nearly always to be found on the outside, representing either portraits, or more often German coats-of-arms (Fig. 24).

Passing over the ordinary glasses, which, with the exception of the style of ornament, are very similar to those which we use (although always of an elongated cylindrical shape), we will occupy our attention only with those enormous drinking glasses (*wiederkommen*) which, if they were mounted on carriages, might be taken for cannons.

Fig. 24.—German Wiederkommen.

We have two such different explanations of the use of the *wiederkommen* in Germany, that we think it necessary to give them both. The following is from Montaigne (*Essais, Liv. ii. Chap.* 2, *de l'Ivrognerie*).

"Anacharsis[*] was surprised that the Greeks at the end of their repast drank out of a larger glass than at the beginning. It is, I imagine, for the same reason that the Germans do it, who, after dinner, commence their regular drinking bouts."

According to these words, the *wiederkommen* would mean nothing else than the cup containing the *coup de grâce*, which each guest took at the end of the repast.

Without pretending to doubt the capacity of the German stomachs, we yet prefer the use dictated by the meaning of the word. The literal translation of the word *wiederkommen* is *to come back*, and we will try to prove the real use by facts themselves.

A *wiederkommen* containing several pints was presented, at the end of a feast, to the host, who after having drunk out of it, passed it to his right-hand neighbor, who in his turn, after having sipped from it, presented it to the next person, and so on, until all the guests, who were generally numerous, had drunk out of the *wiederkommen*, which *came back* to the host empty.

This not very alluring custom, which perhaps

---

[*] Diogenes Laërtius, 'Life of Anacharsis,' i. l.

would be very little appreciated by us,* is still in use at Bruges, for we read in a newspaper of that town:—"In the Flemish taverns, the hostess and the barmaids never serve a full glass without taking a sip from it, and wishing your good health before presenting it to you."

This custom dated back as far as the time of the Spanish sway, and was continued during the civil wars which for so long ravaged that unfortunate country. At that time poison was often concealed at the bottom of the glass. The passing round of the Flemish glass and the *wiederkommen*, which might have had the same origin as the former, was then only, so to say, a momentary assurance of safety given by the host to each of his guests.

Besides, the custom of drinking all round out of the same glass at the beginning of the repast is not modern, for Horace gives us to understand that it was in use in his time, when he speaks of the *coppa magistra* (very large glass).

BOHEMIAN GLASS.

The glass of Bohemia is certainly among the finest that is made at the present day. Although, in order

---

* We have just been told by a German that this custom has been abolished in good society. Only students, at the end of their meals, pass round a large horn filled with wine, from which each one drinks in his turn.

[At some of the dinners of the city companies in London, the custom of passing round a loving-cup still prevails, but this cup is generally of silver, and is always accompanied by a napkin.—TRANSLATOR.]

to display its quality and clearness, it seldom has any external color, it has a style of ornament which is peculiar to itself; we refer to the engraved objects which are observable on a majority of specimens (Fig. 32, p. 167).

In order to avoid useless repetitions we refer our readers to the article on "Cutting and Engraving," &c., where the various processes of engraving on glass will be found fully explained.

VENETIAN AND FRENCH GLASS.

Although the drinking-glasses of Germany appear to have all been formed in the same mould, and in Bohemia the ornamentation is uniformly produced by engraving, this is far from being the case in Italy. For there, thousands of varied shapes show that each artist, imbued entirely with his own individual idea, far from imitating his neighbor's works, endeavors to produce a fantastical, sometimes even an absurd singularity, bordering on the impossible, but nearly always carrying with it that elegance, that stamp of originality, which pleases and fascinates so much.

We will give a few examples of these shapes.

The first (Fig. 25) represents a glass of which the bowl, composed of five bosses, one above another, of gradually increasing dimensions, rests on a stem decorated on each side with a dragon with a crested head of white glass, whose enfolded body is formed of a twisted cane in *latticinio* (eleven inches in height).

Although the middle part of the second specimen

(Fig. 26) is somewhat similar to the former, this re-

Fig. 25.—Venetian Glass.

semblance entirely disappears in the shape, and more especially in the color of the bodies of the dragons. In the former they were milk white, here they are formed by three threads of enamelled yellow, white and red; and the crests of the dragons in the former

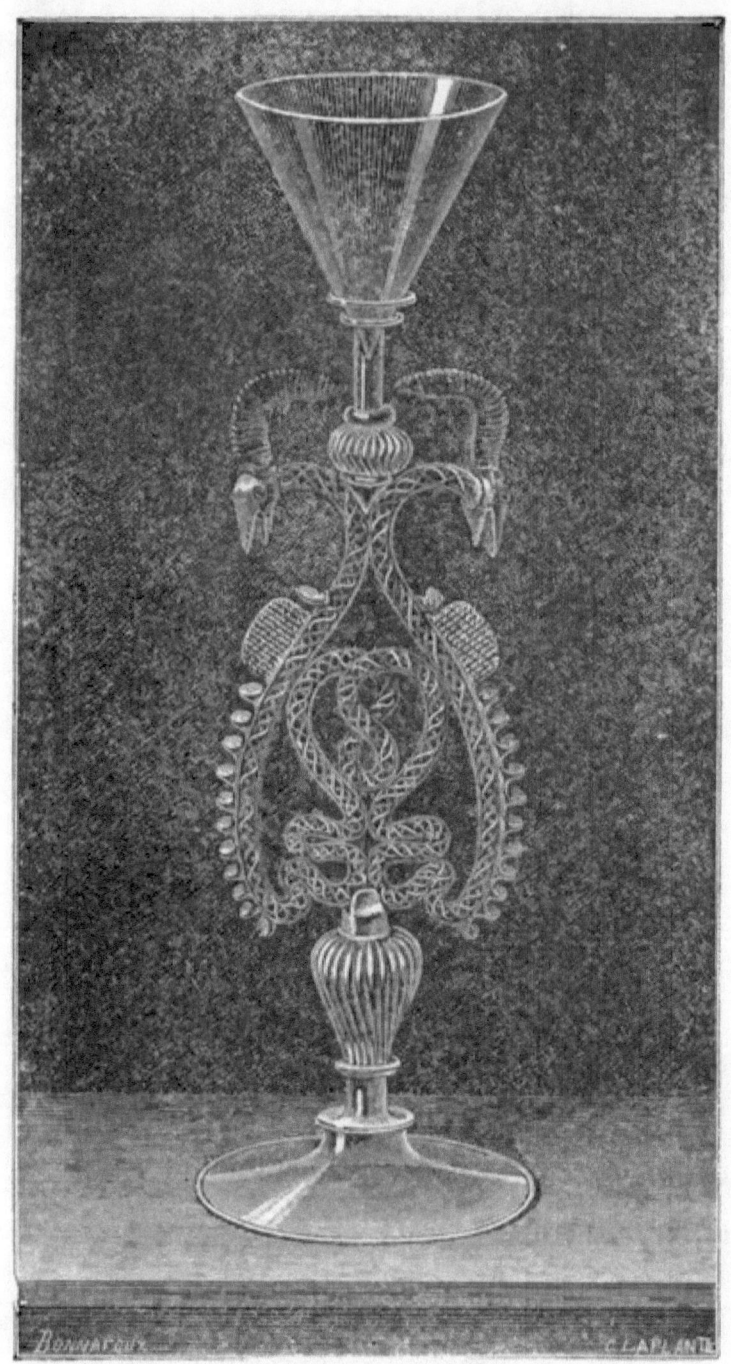

Fig. 26.—Venetian Glass.

are white, while in the latter they are of blue glass.

The third glass (Fig. 27) has no resemblance to the preceding ones; the form is entirely different, the bowl consists of a white glass cup waved by gentle flames of light blue set off by streaks of white; and instead of the dragons, which are almost traditional in Venetian glass, the red and white spiral stem is decorated with a large flower with six projecting petals of a pale blue color, similar to that of the cup, and supported on either side by five large leaves of an opaque yellow glass, separated in the middle by another leaf of a very deep blue color.

In spite of these unquestionable merits, Venetian glass has had and still has calumniators, who reproach it as being not only of little practical utility, but even impossible to use.

If among these objects of art and of curiosity we wished only to find common drinking glasses, such as we ordinarily use, if, in a word, practical use is the sole thing which ought to be valued in this world, then certainly the objections would gain the day; but before entirely condemning such a style of manufacture as this, it is indispensable to know for what use the object has been made. We will endeavor to point out the error on which the reproach against Italian glass rests.

From the distorted shapes, from the excrescence of flower ornaments, from the projecting appendages of animals bearing on their heads large crests made with the *pucellas;* * in short, from the absolute im-

Fig. 27.—Venetian Glass.

possibility of making ordinary use of these glasses,

* The *pucellas* is a pair of tongs used while the glass is still in a soft state.

must we not conclude that the Venetians not only had others of a more common description, but also that those elaborate works of which we have been speaking were at that time what they are now, simply

Fig. 2ª.—Glasses (Crystal Works of Clichy).

ornaments to be placed in cabinets with other curiosities? But between these glasses of very marked originality, and those low and heavy glasses of cylindrical form which we so commonly use, it was **very** desirable to find an intermediate kind, and this **was** the more difficult as the problem was to unite two very distinct qualities of Venetian glass, namely, ornament and use.

In spite of unheard-of difficulties which will always be found when we endeavor to unite these two diametrically opposite aims, it is however impossible to deny that the problem has been solved in modern times; for not satisfied with having substituted clear and light crystal glass for the yellowish glass, filled with streaks and bubbles, of the ancients, the moderns have also learnt how to give to their productions those forms at once pure, slender, and practical, which are the realization of that great vanquished difficulty—useful ornament.

In order to allow the reader to judge for himself whether there is any exaggeration in what we have said, we give an illustration of three glasses as types of this beautiful modern glass, of which however we have already seen one example, in the glass jug on page 137.

Leaving the question of artistic utility to the discernment of the reader, and putting on one side all national strife, we must now combat an oft-repeated assertion—an assertion which goes so far as to deny the origin of the two Venetian glasses represented in Fig. 29, under the very specious pretext that champagne glasses could not have existed in the sixteenth century, for the simple reason that champagne itself did not exist at that period.

One of the glasses is entirely in *latticinio filigree*, cut in diamond pattern; the other, which is colorless, is decorated towards the foot with the body of a fantastic animal.

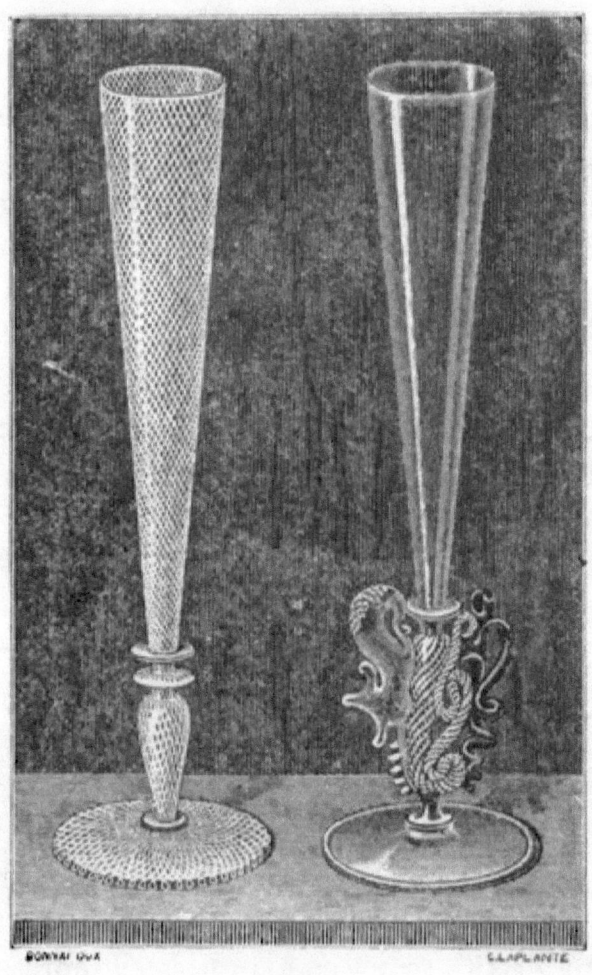

Fig. 29.—Venetian Glass.

The depth of the first is eleven inches, and that of the latter ten inches.

To be able to deny that these high glasses were used in the sixteenth century, it would be necessary to prove that the art of fermenting wine was then unknown, and also that of making effervescing drinks, which it would have been customary, considering their resemblance to our champagne, to drink out of tall glasses. But in order to verify the date of the manufacture of these glasses, which we have styled champagne glasses, it would be sufficient to find even the smallest growth of champagne at that period: this would be enough to baffle our adversaries. We have therefore consulted various writers, and have found the following passage in the work of Coutant d'Orville (*Precis d'une histoire générale de la vie des Francois*, page 66). "In the sixteenth century the wine of Ay was so renowned, that the Emperor Charles V., Pope Leo X., Francis I., and Henry VIII., king of England, sought after this wine as a real nectar; and there is a tradition in the province that each of these great sovereigns bought a piece of ground, with a small house, at Ay, whence a wine-dresser in their employ sent them every year a supply of this rich wine."

There being therefore no longer any doubt either as to the age or the probable or possible use of these two glasses, there only remains to give the reader a specimen of the French art during the sixteenth century. This glass (Fig. 30), which is to be found in the collection bequeathed by the late Mr. Felix Slade to the British Museum, is certainly one of the most remarkable which we know, both as regards its shape and the enamelled painting with which it is decorated.

Fig. 30.—French Glass of the Sixteenth Century.

On the cup is the portrait of a nobleman in the costume of the period of Henry II. of France, who is presenting a bouquet to a lady, and in order that there may be no doubt as to his meaning, we have IE SVIS A VOVS written on a scroll. Not wishing, as it appears, to be behind-hand in courtesy, the lady holds a padlocked heart bearing the following words, MO CŒVR AVES. In a third compartment is a goat (*bouc*), forming an allusive coat of arms, explained over again by the legend round the top part of the glass: IE SVIS A VOVS-JEHAN BOVCAV ET ANTOINETTE BOVC.

The rarity of these glasses, especially those with figures, is explained by two reasons, first, the high price of the painting, secondly, the dissimilarity among them; for these glasses, bearing the portrait and often the arms of the owner, and being only used by him, have very rarely a fellow.

A French proverb, found in Rabelais, "*Toujours souvient à Robin de ses flutes*," * is held to afford presumptive proof that a kind of drinking-glass of large capacity was formerly known as a "flûte," "flûtes" being still a familiar French expression for toping or drinking hard. Robin appears to have been a toper, who prevented by the gout from continuing his former excesses, is unable to forget his old friends, the "flûtes," or capacious drinking vessels.

* 'Livre des proverbes Français,' by Leroux de Lincy, tome ii., p. 61, under ROBIN.

CHAPTER VII.

GILDING ON GLASS.

The means of fixing gold to the outside of a glass were perhaps known and even practised by the ancients, who understood a much more difficult process, namely, how to mix gold with the glass; but in the absence of actual examples of such work, we will content ourselves with giving the method employed at the present time, which, with very little difference, must be the same as that which was formerly used. In order to fix a gilt decoration on a glass, a certain quantity of gold must be dissolved in *aqua-regia*. When the gold is dissolved, the solution is treated either with potash, or better still with sulphate of protoxide of iron. The precipitate which is formed is thrown on a filter, and when mixed with a very small quantity of calcined borax it is reduced to a paste by means of spirits of turpentine.

After this paste has been applied to the glass by a brush, the glass is exposed to the fire of a muffle, which volatilizes the spirits of turpentine and vitrifies the borax.

The gold thus firmly fixed on the glass is burnished first by means of blood-stone, and afterwards with agate.

This method of gilding is, moreover, precisely the same as that used for gilding porcelain. Since we are speaking of gilding as used for ornamenting

Fig. 31.—Venetian Glass sprinkled with Gold.

glass, it will not be out of the way to mention another mode of working, which is very rare and much more difficult to be explained; for although every one agrees as to the manner of the exterior application of gilding, which we have just explained, it is certainly not so with regard to the work of which we are going to speak.

The article in question is a glass jug of Venetian manufacture, which is decorated with particles of gold in the glass (Fig. 31).

The explanation of this kind of work, which, we repeat, is very exceptional, has for a long time engaged the attention of the most competent judges of the matter, and up to the present time doubt still exists; for, according to some, the gold was mixed with the vitreous paste when it was still in the crucible, whilst, according to others, the gold dust was not sprinkled over the glass until it had been blown into shape.

Since the subject is still open to discussion, we may be allowed to give our opinion on one point, which we think has not been sufficiently considered, viz., the complete smoothness of the vase.

If we admit that the gold was simply applied to the glass whilst it was still malleable, there must necessarily have resulted a certain appreciable unevenness, if not to the sight at least to the touch.

As the vase in question has not the slightest roughness, we must endeavor to find out in what manner this surface can have been made so smooth, that no unevenness whatever can be felt.

There are two ways of producing this result, which, although they are different in execution, produce the same result. The one consists in sprinkling gold dust over the lump of glass the moment the shape is obtained, whilst the other is by rolling this same lump of glass on a marver covered with gold dust.

The lump of glass being covered with gold by either of these processes, we have only to explain by what means gold may be rendered imperceptible to the touch. This appears to us to consist solely in a covering of very fine transparent glass, which, applied to the outside of the glass, encloses, so to speak, the gold dust between two casings.

It is useless for us to enlarge further on this easy process, which is employed at the present time in the manufacture of glass of several colors, called double glass. (See the chapter on Glass of Two Layers, page 173.)

CHAPTER VIII.

GLASS CUTTING AND ENGRAVING.

We have previously seen that the art of moulding, cutting, and engraving crystal glass dates back to a very remote period, for Pliny (Book xxxvi., Chap. 66) tells us that "sometimes glass was blown, sometimes fashioned on a wheel, and sometimes chased like silver."

The antiquity of this art being thus ascertained, let us pass over many centuries and come to the present time, in order to see what means are employed in our days.

I.—GLASS CUTTING.

Glass cutting, which generally consists in the production of ornaments in relief on the outside, is done by means of four vertical wheels which are successively used, and are set in motion either by the workman's foot or by steam power. The first of these wheels is made of iron, the second of sandstone, the third of wood, and the fourth of cork.

On the iron wheel when set in motion, the workman throws from time to time some sand, which is moistened by means of a little wooden trough placed above the wheel, which lets water drop on to the sand.

The first operation of rough cutting being finished, the iron wheel is succeeded by the sandstone wheel, which is more lightly applied, and adds another degree to the process of cutting. This wheel is then followed by the wooden one, on which the workmen throw by turns, sand pulverised by the two preceding operations, very fine emery,* and lastly putty powder.†

The process of cutting is finished either by the same wooden wheel sprinkled with dry tin putty and covered with a piece of woollen stuff, or by means of the last wheel of cork.

As we have seen then, the cutting of glass is done by grinding it either on the plane and lateral sides, on the cylindrical part, or even on the edges of the wheels whilst in motion.

In consequence of the process of decoration costing, as is seen, a very great amount of labor, cut glasses are always very dear, and for this reason a cheaper method has been discovered by which they can be roughly imitated. The following is the process employed in order to obtain this economical result. The glass is first blown in a mould, having

---

* This mineral, principally composed of alumina, takes its name from the Cape Emery (Isle of Naxos), where it is extracted in considerable quantities.

† Putty powder is a mixture of oxide of lead and tin.

inside the design which is required, and the cast thus obtained is finished on the wheel.

It can be understood that by this process the costly labor of cutting being very much advanced by the moulding, the manufacturer obtains a very great economy in time, labor, and even material, which allows him to offer to the public objects at a relatively moderate price.

II.—ENGRAVING ON GLASS.

Although engraving on glass produces a result precisely opposite to cutting, since the work of the former is cut in, whilst by that of the latter ornaments in relief are generally produced, the manner of execution is very similar; for both are executed by the aid of a wheel, with certain differences, which we think it necessary to mention.

Instead of using the wheels which, in the cutting, grind the glass, the engraver of glass employs a spindle which, terminating in either a tempered steel or flint point, is fixed to a small drum worked by a crank. When set in motion the workman takes the object which he wishes to engrave, and following the outlines of the design lightly traced out, he presses the glass more or less against the point of the spindle, according to the depth of the engraving required.

The difficulties of this work, which, as may be imagined, requires great sleight of hand added to long practice, can only be appreciated when those works are closely examined on which the artist has engraved the most complicated scenes on a very small space.

It will be well to mention here what M. Labarte says on this art:—

"From the commencement of the seventeenth century, certain glass manufactories in Bohemia produced vases of a correct shape enriched with engraved ornaments, representing scenes and very frequently portraits.

"Distinguished artists were employed in Germany and Italy, in spite of the fragility of the material, to decorate these vases, in imitation of those in rock crystal, with ornaments and arabesque subjects, remarkable for their composition, their purity of design, and their elaborate execution. Many of these beautiful engravings deserved to have been made on a less fragile material."

Whilst stating here that the art of engraving on glass has been brought, like all hand labor, to a very high degree of perfection by the Bohemian artists, it must yet be acknowledged that amongst their most beautiful productions a certain degree of monotony is always to be found, resulting in a great measure from the multiplicity of lines engraved so close to one another, that it might almost be thought that the talent of the engraver consisted in placing the greatest amount of engraving in the least possible space. It certainly shows a relative talent; but was

Fig. 32.—Bohemian Glass.

the aim of engraving on glass, namely, to decorate, attained? The French artists thought not, and abandoning the Bohemian compositions, they substituted for the castles, the nobles, and peasants with their microscopical sheep, interlaced flowers, which, by

Fig. 33.—Engraved Flagon (Clichy Glass Works).

their varied compositions, offer, as may be conceived, much more pleasing and luminous effects, and create, so to speak, a new art.

The engraving which we give (Fig. 33) and which

doubtless supports what we have said, is a copy of a little flagon emanating from the glass works at Clichy.

We have seen that manufacturers succeeded in making cut glasses popular by means of a preliminary blowing; there are also imitations of engraved glasses, and the following is the method of making them, as described by M. Péligot.

"In order to engrave on glass, fluoric acid is employed in either a gaseous or liquid state. It is preferable to use it in the latter form. The fluoric acid is prepared by the ordinary process, by heating in a *leaden retort* one part of pulverised fluoride of calcium and three and a half parts of concentrated sulphuric acid. The acid is diluted by a third or half of its volume of water, and is kept in bottles of lead, or, what is better, gutta-percha.

"The glass is coated with a varnish of wax and turpentine, which is applied hot by means of a brush. For designs which should present a certain amount of fineness, drying linseed oil is used.

"The design is traced with a point, in the same manner as etching. The transparency of the varnish of linseed oil permits it to be easily traced. The part covered with varnish is coated with wax, and the acid is allowed to eat into the glass for a long or short period, according to the depth of the engraving required.* The varnish is removed by washing it in water and then in diluted alcohol. It is unnecessary

* Douze leçons sur l'Art de la Verrerie, page 19.

to add that the glass is only touched in those parts which have been laid bare by the engraver."

As it is impossible, whatever amount of care may be taken in this chemical operation, that every part eaten by the acid should have the sharpness and clearness of line given by the point of the tool, it will always be easy to distinguish the work done by the hand of man from that done by the acid.

Thanks to M. Péligot, the question concerning these imitations of Bohemian glass being settled, let us mention, still under the guidance of this writer, those other glasses which, as they are decorated with light designs in imitation of muslin or lace, cannot on account of their extreme regularity be made by the hand.

CHAPTER IX.

LACE GLASS.

"M. Gugnon, of Metz, applies to the glass, covered with a very light coating of essence of turpentine, an open-work design in metal or on paper, representing lace, &c. He then sifts a fine powder of asphalte and mastic over its surface. The pattern is then carefully taken off, and the glass is slightly heated, so as to melt the powder spread in the interstices of the design, which are thus preserved from the action of the acid, which is now allowed to eat into the glass during thirty or forty minutes, and only takes effect on that part of the glass to which the pattern of the design had adhered.

"This process is very rapid, and by these means two workmen can engrave in a day about twenty superficial yards of glass."

CHAPTER X.

ON GLASS COMPOSED OF TWO LAYERS.

Up to the present time we have only spoken of glass which is throughout of the same color.

The skill of the ancients however did not stop there, for not content with being able to produce precious stones in artificial monochromes, they even became able to imitate one of the most rare works of creation, the onyx, which, as is well known, is a stone composed of two or three layers of different colors. The Louvre collection possesses several splendid objects of this description, extremely rare and not to be found now-a-days.

Before placing before the reader the illustration of the Portland Vase, which is the most beautiful example known of glass of two layers, and before narrating the history and misfortunes of this chef-d'œuvre, let us say a word on the method employed in obtaining glass with two distinct layers. If a glass-maker wishes to make a vase or anything of the kind with alternate white and red streaks, he begins by taking on the end of his blowing iron a small quantity of white glass which he rolls on the marver.

This being done, he then dips this white glass into a pot containing red glass in a state of fusion; this latter glass being thus finely coated over the former, the workman blows the object, and gives whatever form he wishes to it.

When this is finished, the next thing to be done is to make the white glass partially reappear, which has been totally hidden by the red.

This operation presents, as the reader has doubtless already foreseen, a very great resemblance to engraving on glass (page 165). In the latter process the work consists of tracing a design by cutting away a part of the vitreous matter; in the former, where the glass is composed of two layers, the method is exactly the same, since it is only necessary to remove certain portions of the outer layer in order to make the under one reappear. The resemblance of these two processes is the more remarkable as the three same agents, namely, the flint, the wheel, and fluoric acid, are used in each of these arts.

As regards the method of cutting away by flint and the wheel, and eating away by acid, the reader will understand, without it being necessary for us to explain, that, in the two former processes the flint and wheel only touch those parts which are to be taken away; and also, that in the process with the acid, these are the only parts which, as in engraving on glass, are not coated with a varnish of wax and turpentine to neutralize the incisive effect of the acid.

We could not better conclude this chapter on

glass of two layers than by giving a description of that wonder of wonders, the vase designated by the archæologists successively under the names of the Barberini and the Portland Vase (Fig. 34).

A few words will explain the origin of the two names. This vase, found about the sixteenth century in a marble sarcophagus in the environs of Rome, after having been for more than two centuries the principal ornament in the gallery of the Princes Barberini at Rome, was bought at a sale by auction by the Duchess of Portland, for the sum of eighteen hundred and seventy-two pounds.

Although the legitimate and sole proprietress of this chef-d'œuvre, the duchess, who doubtless did not recognize the right of hiding from public admiration such a unique object, lent this vase to the British Museum, where it is still to be seen. Thus it was preserved, admired by all the world. One day, however, there nearly remained nothing more than the resemblance of it, for a lunatic named Lloyd smashed it in pieces by the blow of a stick. This injury, committed by a madman, was repaired by an artist in such a manner and with such skilfulness, that it is impossible to distinguish the numerous places where it is joined together.

This unique vase, which is supposed to have been made in the time of the Antonines (about 138 years B.C.), is composed of layers of glass one over the other. The lower one is of a deep blue color and the other of opaque white, so that the figures stand out in white on a deep blue back-ground.

These two layers lying one over the other so much resemble an onyx,* that for a long time the archæologists described this vase as being an ancient cameo;† whilst it is now well known that it is, as we have just said, a glass vase composed of two layers.

But although the material is perfectly known, we cannot say as much regarding the subject which it represents, as authorities still differ on this point. We will quote here what Millingen says with regard to it in his *Monuments inédits*, vol. i., page 27.

"The Portland vase represents (No. 1) the marriage of Peleus and Thetis. The woman seated, holding a serpent in her left hand, is Thetis, and the man to whom she is giving her right hand is Peleus. The serpent recalls the different transformations by means of which she reckoned upon escaping marriage. The god placed in front of Thetis is Neptune. A Cupid hovering above them in the air unites the two lovers. The portico behind Peleus probably signifies the palace of that prince, or else the sanctuary in which Thetis received divine honors.

"On the reverse (No. 2) Thetis is again seen seated, holding a torch downwards, an emblem of sleep.

---

* From the Greek ὄνυξ, finger-nail. A species of very fine agate which is composed of parallel layers of different colors, one of which resembles the milky color of the nail.

† From the Italian *cameo*, a stone composed of different colors and engraved in relief.

Fig. 34.—Portland Vase.

The man seated at her feet is Peleus; the other figure with a lance in his hand is the nymph of Mount Pelion, where the scene takes place."

Under the frieze we give a bust (No. 3) which is placed beneath the foot of the vase, and omitted by Millingen; it represents Ganymede (?).

On each side of this bust are copies of the masks on the handles.

CHAPTER XI

THE IRIDESCENCE OF GLASS.

Public opinion generally attributes that charming opalescent and nacreous play of color which we see on a great many specimens of antique glass to the action of accidental fire, and there are few who do not consider each piece a rare and fragile survivor of the Pompeian catastrophe.

In order to prove that fire has nothing to do with this iridescence, it will suffice to remind the reader of the fact that the greater part, or even all the antique glass which adorns our museums, came from the tombs, where it had been placed beside the arms, jewellery, and garments of the dead.

The presence of garments and jewellery which bear no signs of any alteration forbids all idea of fire: we must therefore endeavor to find elsewhere the cause of this iridescence. Here again M. Péligot comes to our aid. "The majority of glass objects," says he, " whose manufacture dates back to a remote period, have undergone, by the influence of time and damp, a very marked alteration. All the old glass which is found in the tombs of the ancient Romans and Gauls presents an iridescent and black aspect, giving sometimes very brilliant reflections, like those of the wings of certain species of butterflies. It is to be found even on panes of glass of more modern manufacture placed in the windows of stables, etc., viz., places often exposed both to constant damp and high temperature. The iridescent scales, which can be easily removed by gentle rubbing, are a mixture of silica and earthly silicates, the alkaline silicates having disappeared."

CHAPTER XII.

FROSTED GLASS.

This name is given to a species of glass or crystal invented in Bohemia and formerly much used in Italy; it imitates as well as possible, by means of external roughness, the fine arabesques of the thin coating of ice which in winter nights covers the windows of a room mildly heated in the interior.

Before describing the process of the manufacture of this glass, we may be allowed to show the reader a Venetian goblet (Fig. 35) which, from its elegant shape and decorated style, rich as well as chaste in ornamentation, is certainly one of the most faultless products of the glass works of Murano; for, as we are about to show, it is the result of several different operations. Indeed, this goblet with eight lobes is composed of two equal and horizontal zones; the upper one, blown and moulded, is decorated at the top by a wide gilded border, whilst the lower one of frosted glass rests on a moulded and gilded pedestal.

This kind of glass is now usually employed in the manufacture of the decanters, known under the name of *brocs à glaces.*

FROSTED GLASS.

This frosted glass, so original in its appearance, was long and rightly used merely in white glass, which color imitates natural ice better than any other. But ignorant, or perhaps forgetful that this glass representing ice was only an indication, a label, so to speak, serving to indicate that what the decan-

Fig. 35.—Venetian Frosted Glass (Louvre).

ter contained was frozen, fashion decreed that it was tired of the white ice of nature, and required some of another color. Fashion gave the order, and then it was that manufacturers invented frosted glass in yellow, green, lilac, pink, etc.

The mode of manufacture employed to obtain this frosted appearance, astonishing as it may appear, is, as we shall see, very simple. A piece of glass, white or colored in the mass, being taken from the pot, is placed on a molten or iron table on which fragments of pounded glass have been placed. These fragments adhering to the exterior of the glass whilst that is still soft, it is again heated, and finally blown.

It will be understood that the fragments of glass being only attached to the exterior, the interior of the objects in frosted glass is quite smooth.

There is yet another method employed in Bohemia, which may be called artistic frosting, for its system of ornament is susceptible of infinite varieties, as it depends entirely on the will of the maker; whilst that of which we have spoken above, from the manner of its fabrication can only represent a monochromatic frosting, general and without any settled design.

This is the process employed to obtain the artistic frosting.

Instead of rolling the glass when it is still without form on a layer of pounded glass, the object in course of making is blown, and it is only when it is nearly completed that the artist, who has pounded glass of different colors before him, puts it *with his hand* wherever he desires on the glass when still in a pasty state.

From this system it follows that the decoration of the glass is quite under the control of the artist's taste.

This work completed, it only remains to heat the object again and finish it off.

It is needless to say that in both methods, the fragments of glass placed upon the other, being less fusible than the glass to which they adhere, the external roughness is not smoothed down by the second heating of the glass.

CHAPTER XIII.

SPUN GLASS.

WHICH of you, dear readers (I am only speaking to those who have seen their fiftieth year), does not remember, when he was a child, having admired little houses, sheepfolds with shepherd, shepherdess, and sheep, and even castles, constructed entirely of glass threads of different colors?

The fashion for this sort of toy, we dare not say work of art, has already fallen into what everything else must come to, the most complete oblivion; and its abandonment is so great that it would be easier now for some persons to purchase a house of hewn stone costing three or four thousand pounds, than to lay their hand on a little glass house.

As we are not, thank God, amongst those who cry *væ victis!* we think that in gratitude for the happiness and wonder this sort of work has caused us, we must at least endeavor to show here that spun glass has had its reign, and to prove that in skilful hands it may still possess an artistic interest.

Is spun glass of modern invention? Alas! not more so than many other things here below. At the

Fig. 36.—Spun Glass (Louvre).

beginning of this century it was only a continuation of a manufacture which had been long known, and had been so much esteemed in the commencement of the sixteenth century, that Fugger, the rich banker of Augsburg, who, not content with warming his guest, Charles V., with bundles of cinnamon wood, lighted them with the bond for a large sum which the sovereign had borrowed from him, found nothing rarer or more worthy of being offered to his imperial visitor than a small vessel of molten, spun, cast, and twisted glass.

From the great resemblance between this description and an object in the Louvre (Fig. 36), it would be easy to give this vessel an historical interest; but that not being a question for us, we will content ourselves with having shown the antiquity of spun glass and the esteem in which it was held, and will pass at once to the method of its manufacture.

If we go into the workroom of the pearl-blower (Chap. XXIV.), we shall see him seated at a little table on which his tubes are placed, and a lamp giving a long jet of flame. Precisely the same apparatus is required by the glass spinner, although the two works are very different, since the former workman has to produce by his breath little balls which are to become round or ovoid beads, whilst that of the spinner, on the contrary, is merely to obtain from a glass tube fine and flexible thread.

The following process is employed to attain this result. The spinner having chosen a tube, either white or colored, brings one of its extremities to the lamp. As soon as this part of the tube begins to soften, the workman seizes it with small pincers, and stretching out his arms he obtains, owing to the ductility of the glass, a thread about a yard long, adhering on one side to the principal tube, and on the other to the small piece taken off by the pincers.

The spun glass would be limited to this length of about a yard if means had not been discovered to prolong it almost indefinitely. This is done by fixing the extremity of the glass adhering to the pincers to a small wheel or drum of sheet iron, which is set in movement and placed at a short distance from the lamp. Again heated, the principal tube, which is gradually brought nearer the flame, yields in its turn to the traction on it, and soon this fine thread, winding itself round the drum, attains an extraordinary length. Now that our little sheepfolds, so much regretted, no longer exist, we shall doubtless be asked of what use these glass threads can be? They are employed in numerous ways. The glittering dresses which were formerly worn were made of silk and glass threads woven together. The aigrets also which ornament ladies' bonnets, and are so fine and flexible that the lightest breeze agitates them, are of spun glass. The flowing black curls, which, when worn by a prince, became the admiration of all Paris, were likewise made of spun glass, curled with irons.

Many readers will probably doubt the truth of our statements, thinking it impossible that such things could be produced in glass. But let the incredulous go to the *Conservatoire des Arts et Métiers* at Paris, and there, in the glass room, they will see a lion of the size of life, with splendid hair and bristling mane, stifling a serpent.* Convinced by sight, they will then acknowledge that in skilful hands spun glass may produce effects wonderful, not only from their delicacy, but also from the richness and truth of their colors.

The *Dictionnaire des arts et manufactures* speaks thus of this group and its author. "A very clever enameller of Saumur has made an extremely interesting application of threads of spun glass, using it to imitate the hair of animals. He assimilates the colors to those of natural skins, and after having cut the threads of a suitable length, he attaches them by one end on a solid surface, copying the arrangement of the skin that he wishes to imitate. I have seen at his house tigers, striped hyenas, and other animals of natural size, admirably modelled and covered with the *glass hair* of which we speak.

"The imitation is so perfect, that these animals might advantageously replace the stuffed skins, always injured, which encumber our museums."

If the idea of imitating the hair of animals with glass threads is a modern invention, it is certainly not the case with materials woven with glass, for we find in the *Mémoires de l'Académie des Sciences* (1713),

---

* This group, which cost its author, M. Lambourg, thirty years' labor, formed a part of the Universal Exhibition of 1855.

a report of the celebrated Réaumur,* in which he says: "If they succeed in making glass threads as fine as those of spiders' webs, they will have glass threads of which woven stuffs may be made."

What was then only a contingent possibility for the *savant* has since become a reality. Thanks to modern industry, glass is now drawn as fine and flexible as the finest thread of the silkworm.

Before concluding this notice of spun glass, it may be as well to contradict an error held by many people, who deny that a hollow tube can be lengthened without destroying the bore. We borrow the proof to the contrary from the *Dictionnaire technologique des arts* (Vol. xxii., page 216). "When a hollow tube of glass is drawn out, the hole remains, whatever may be the fineness of the thread. M. Deuchar took a piece of thermometer tube, the interior diameter of which was very small, and drew it out into threads. The drum which he employed was three feet in circumference, and as it turned round five hundred times in a minute, 30,000 yards of thread were obtained in an hour, so that the thread was extremely fine, and its interior diameter scarcely calculable. This thread was, however, hollow, for being cut into pieces of an inch and a half in length, and placed in the receiver of an air-pump, with one end inside and the other out, it allowed the mercury to

---

* René-Antoine Ferchault de Réaumur, physician and naturalist, born at Rochelle, in 1683, died in 1757. He was named member of the Académie des Sciences in 1708.

pass in small shining filaments as soon as a vacuum was made."

As we have just mentioned the words thermometer and tubes, we will see as succinctly as possible how the tube of a thermometer is made, and by what means the mercury or alcohol is introduced.

CHAPTER XIV.

ON THE THERMOMETER AND ITS ORIGIN.

EVERY one knows that the thermometer, as its name indicates, serves to measure the different variations of temperature. It is generally composed of a plate marking by its equal divisions the various degrees of heat and cold. In the middle is a cylindrical and perpendicular glass tube of small diameter, having in the interior a small quantity of mercury, or spirits of wine colored with carmine, either of which stopping at one of the divisions indicated on the plate, marks the successive fluctuations of the temperature.

According to M. Libri,[*] the invention of the thermometer is due to Galileo;[†] according to other authors to Francis Bacon,[‡] to Fludd,[§] to Drebbel,[‖]

---

[*] "*Histoire des Sciences Math' matiques, en Italie,*" vol. iv., page 189.

[†] Galileo Galilei, born at Pisa, 1564, died 1642.

[‡] F. Bacon, born at London, 1561, died 1626.

[§] Fludd (Robert), physician, born at Milgate, in Kent, 1574, died 1637.

[‖] Drebbel (Cornelius van), born at Alckmaer (Holland), 1572, died 1634.

or, lastly, to Sanctorius.* The most general opinion ascribes it to Cornelius Drebbel; and yet to this long list of supposed inventors, M. Hoefer † adds a fresh competitor, Van Helmont, who, according to this gentleman, must have originated the idea of the construction of a thermometer. We give the words of M. Hoefer verbatim.

"Van Helmont, indignant that a certain Heer should reproach him with having pursued the chimera of perpetual motion, said that he had made use of an instrument of his own invention, not to seek perpetual motion, but to prove that water enclosed in a hollow tube of glass, terminated by a ball, rises and falls according to the temperature of the surrounding medium. This idea thrown out by chance was one day to be fertile in results."

If the absence of proofs leaves the name of the inventor of the thermometer still undetermined, we are more fortunate in regard to the date of its appearance, for it is generally agreed that the first appeared in Germany, under the name of Cornelius Drebbel, in 1621.

Although the thermometer was from that time known and even in use, it must still have been, from the descriptions we have of it, very far from that state of perfection to which it has attained in our times.

* Sanctorius, the latinized name of Santori, a celebrated physician born at Capo d'Istria 1561, died 1636.

† *Dictionnaire de Chimie*, at the word *Thermometer*.

Those successive ameliorations and improvements, arising from the ever-progressive march of science, have been related by M. Figuier,* in his book on *Grandes inventions, anciennes et modernes*

MANUFACTURE OF THE TUBES.

Like everything in glass, tubes are made by the breath of the workman. If the reader will kindly

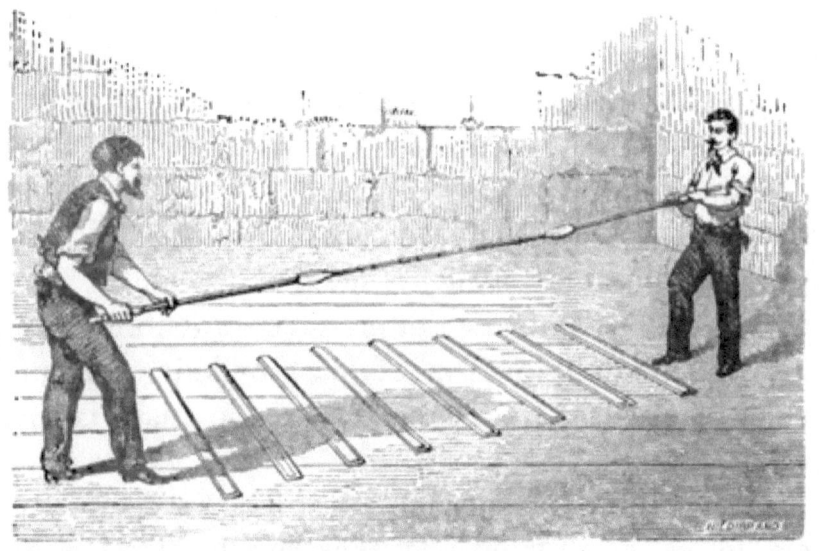

Fig. 37.—Drawing out a Glass Tube.

look once more at the plate representing the blowing of a glass globe destined to become a window pane, he will have an exact idea of the first stage in the formation of tubes.

As soon as the workman has blown a ball of the size desired, another workman fastens his ponty to

* Paris, Hachette, 1861, page 131.

the side opposite that adhering to the pipe of the blower, and he walks quickly backwards whilst the blower remains in the same place. Thanks to the malleability and ductility of the glass, softened by the heat, this globe, according to the traction given it, is lengthened to such a degree that it becomes a long tube.

It will be seen that the ball blown being hollow, the tube formed from it preserves also in its centre a continuous and equal cavity in proportion with the diameter given to the tube. (See what is said of this in the article on Spun Glass, page 192.)

To avoid returning to this subject, and before giving our entire attention to tubes destined for thermometers, we may mention that all straight tubes are made in the same manner; but that the spiral tubes used in chemistry, which often have serpentine forms, are obtained by means of cast cylinders, around which the tubes are wound whilst the glass is malleable.

As for the tubes specially destined for thermometers, let us see in what way they can be filled either with mercury or alcohol.

The capillarity * of the tube, but still more the resistance offered by the air it contains, renders the direct introduction, either of the mercury or the alcohol, impossible. This resistance has therefore to be

---

* By capillary, from the Latin *capillus*, a hair, is designated a tube whose interior bore is not larger than a hair.

destroyed by heating, with a spirit lamp, the still empty reservoir * of the tube.

Nearly all the air being driven out by this first operation, the open extremity of the tube at the end opposite to the reservoir is then plunged into mercury or alcohol, and as soon as the force of the atmospheric air is greater than that of the small amount of air which remains in the tube, it weighs on the mercury or the alcohol, which by this pression rises in the tube.

Fig. 38.

As soon as a portion of the mercury or alcohol has entered the tube, it is taken up, and then, meeting no more resistance, the mercury or alcohol falls from its own weight into the reservoir, which is then again heated sufficiently to cause the vapors of the substance contained in the reservoir to drive out completely all the air that might remain in the tube.

This operation terminated, the open part of the tube is closed by means of a lamp, and it only remains to graduate it.

* The reservoir, whether spherical or elongated, is a part added to the tube after the latter is made.

THE THERMOMETER AND ITS ORIGIN.

GRADUATION OF TUBES

The place of the lowest mark indicating cold, and denoted on the thermometer by a zero, is determined by means of melting ice. The tube is placed up to the middle in a cylindrical recipient filled with pounded ice. (Fig. 39.)

After it has remained there about a quarter of an

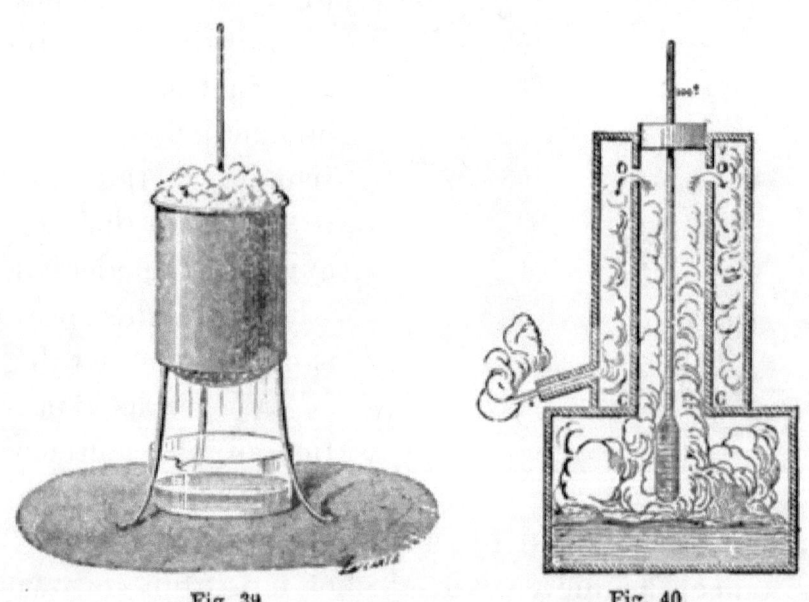

Fig. 39.   Fig. 40.

hour, a line is traced with a diamond on the exact place where the mercury or alcohol stopped. This sign indicates the zero of the thermometer.

It may be easily understood how by a contrary process the degrees of heat are marked. The tube is placed in a stove with the steam of boiling water, and the point at which the mercury stops becomes the hundredth degree of the thermometric scale.* (Fig. 40.)

What we have said about the thermometer has been solely intended to explain the manufacture of tubes in general and the relative importance of glass in the sciences: we should merely repeat ourselves in speaking of the barometer.

* [In Fahrenheit's scale, freezing point is 32° and boiling point 212°—Translator.]

CHAPTER XV.

ON JET.

There are two sorts of jet, one natural, which is classed in the family of the lignites (coal), and is of an intense black, of fine and close texture; the other, artificial, which taken alone offers the form of a small cylindrical black glass tube, obtained, according to M. Péligot, by a mixture of oxide of copper, cobalt, and iron.

Although our intention is merely to treat of artificial jet, the only one in vogue at present, we must say one word on natural jet; which, if it is now forgotten, has also had its time of glory, for we cannot forget that the statue of Menelaus, carried off from the temple of Heliopolis and transported to Rome during the reign of Tiberias, was formed of jet.

Now that we have paid, although certainly very briefly, our debt to antiquity, let us examine if the fashion for artificial jet, employed in our days with so much prodigality as ornaments for dresses, mantles, and bonnets, is a new conception.

Although at the risk of being accused of indulg

ing a mania for antiquity, at the risk too of wounding the national self-love, or of even destroying the fame of certain patents, we shall endeavor to prove that jet embroidery as it is now worn, far from being an innovation, is only a pale and economical imitation of past fashions.

This is what Savary wrote in 1723, in his *Dictionnaire Universel du Commerce*. "It is with artificial jet, cut and pierced, and threaded with silk or thread, that embroideries are made in sufficiently good taste, but very dear, which are used particularly for ornaments in churches. Trimmings are also made of it in half mourning for men and women, and sometimes muffs, tippets, and *trimmings for robes*. For the latter the jet used is white and black, but of whatever color it may be, it is ill employed."

From these words it would be wrong to argue that jet embroidery only goes back to the period indicated by Savary, for the eighteenth century as well as our own lived on the dead, whose inventions it revived. A single example chosen from amongst a thousand will prove this. Let us open the inventory drawn up after the death of Gabrielle d'Estrées (1599), and we shall find a proof that jet was already in fashion. "Five small caps of black satin, of which two are embroidered in jet, one quite full; a robe of black satin, with a border of jet over the body and the sleeves open; valued at forty crowns."

"What matters the precise date of this mode with which we have endowed the whole of Europe?" will say some patentee. "Is it not sufficient for our honor that it is of French origin?"

But this is a fresh error, for not only does the invention not belong to the sixteenth century any more than to the eighteenth, but again, it is not more French than English or German, and to discover its true origin—by this word we speak of that only as-

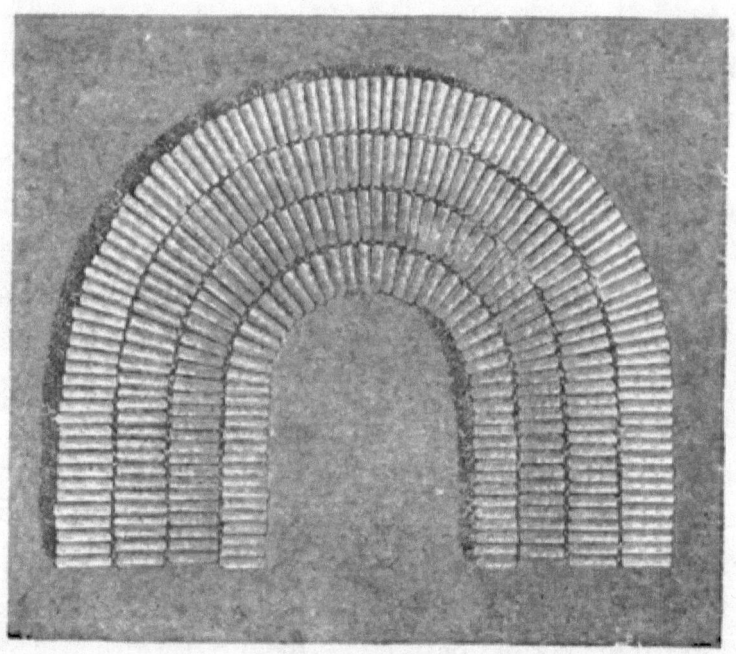

Fig. 41.—Egyptian Breastplate (Louvre).

signed by documents which have come down to us, and not of the invention itself, which is certainly far more ancient—we must go back to the old Egypt of the Pharaohs.

To be convinced of this truth, it is only necessary to look at the sumptuous objects in the Egyptian

Museum in the Louvre. If we examine either the objects themselves, or those painted on the sarcophagi, we shall find a large number of small cylinders, some of enamelled earth, others of colored glass, which although they are in every respect identical with ours in form and use, yet differ essentially in the variety of the colors, which enabled the Egyptian women to compose those charming necklaces and splendid breastplates, so rich in varied effects that one might almost say that in their hands a box of tubes became a palette.

CHAPTER XVI.

BEADS FOR NECKLACES, BRACELETS, AND CHAPLETS.

The manufacture of beads for necklaces, bracelets, and chaplets, whilst presenting great similarity to that of jet, in as much as both are produced from tubes of colorless or colored glass pierced through the centre, yet differ in one particular; as the former are simple oblong tubes, while the others must from their destination receive a form more or less spheroidal.

It is this latter work that we are about to describe.

The tubes, of a diameter proportioned to that of the beads which are required, are at first cut into cylinders of a height equal to their diameter, and are then placed in a pear-shaped drum of beaten iron containing a mixture of plaster and plumbago or of charcoal dust mixed with clay. The drum being placed on a furnace, the workman gives it a continuous rotatory movement by means of an iron axle which passes through it, so that the tubes softened by the heat lose the salient parts of their extremities, from the constant friction with each other, and take a spherical form.

The office of the plaster and charcoal in this work

is to prevent the tubes, at the time of the softening of the glass, from adhering together.

When cool, the tubes are taken out of the drum and sifted, in order to shake out the pulverized matters which have entered.

CHAPTER XVII.

ON THE COLORING OF GLASS AND CRYSTAL.

THE art of coloring glass, which necessarily implies a certain knowledge of chemistry, erroneously denied to the ancients, goes back to an unknown time.

M. Boudet, the author of an excellent work on the art of glass-making in Egypt,* informs us " that the priests of Egypt, who were constantly occupied with experiments, made in their laboratory some glass equal to rock crystal; and profiting by the property they had discovered in oxides of metallic substances obtained principally from India, to vitrify under different colors, they conceived and executed the project of imitating every species of precious stone, whether colored, transparent, or opaque, furnished to them by the commerce of the same country.

"Strabo† and all historians agree in asserting

---

* *Description de l'Egypte*, 2nd edit., Panckoucke, 1829, vol. ix., page 213.

† This Greek geographer, born at Amasia, in Cappadocia, 50 B.C., lived for a long time in Egypt.

that in Egypt, from time immemorial, there were manufactured by secret processes some very fine and very transparent glasses, whose colors were those of the hyacinth, the sapphire, the ruby, etc.; that one of the sovereigns of that country had succeeded in imitating the precious stone named Cyanus; that Sesostris * had caused to be founded or sculptured in glass of emerald color, a statue which was still seen at Constantinople under the reign of Theodosius; that in the time of Apion † there also existed a glass colossus in the labyrinth of Egypt; lastly, Pliny says that with the dross of metals there was made a black glass which resembled the substance of jet, which was employed before it was thought of replacing it by glass.

"Does it require more to prove that the Egyptians are the most ancient fabricators of glass, and that, as they imitated precious stones, they knew how to prepare the oxides without which they could not have succeeded in making colored glasses, false jewels, and enamels?"

There exists such a connexion in the coloring parts, as well as in the method of manufacture of glass and colored crystal, that, to keep within the limits assigned us, and still more to spare the reader tiresome as well as useless repetitions, we must now, having proved the antiquity of colored glass, occupy

---

* Sesostris, or Rameses, began to reign in Egypt about 1643 years B. C.

† A grammarian, born at Oasis, in Egypt, about 40 years B.C.

ourselves especially with false stones considered as an object of adornment.

The imitation of precious stones, first in glass and then in crystal, goes back, as we have just said, to an indefinite period; for we find this art employed by the Egyptians, not only in the enamelled coverings of their innumerable scarabæi, and in those of their long lines of statuettes, but also in the decoration of a number of trinkets, such as earrings and bracelets, where the paste of colored glass is united to the purest gold.

Herodotus* (Book ii., Chap. 69) tells us: "Some of the Egyptians look upon crocodiles as sacred animals. Those who live near Thebes and lake Mœris hold these animals in much veneration. They select one and teach him to allow himself to be touched by the hand. They put on him earrings of gold or of artificial stone, and fasten to his feet little golden chains."

From Egypt this science passed to Rome, for although Pliny (Book xxxvii., Chap. 75) does not indicate the process employed in the manufacture, he mentions the extraordinary skill which the makers of false stones had attained in his time. "There is considerable difficulty in distinguishing genuine stones from false; the more so as there has been discovered a method of transforming genuine stones of one kind into false stones of another. Sardonyx, for example,

---

* Herodotus, who deserves the surname of *Father of History*, was born at Halicarnassus, 484 B.C.

is imitated by cementing together three other precious stones, in such a way that no skill can detect the fraud; a black stone being used for the purpose, a white stone and one of a vermilion color, each of them, in its way, a stone of high repute. Nay, even more than this, there are books in existence, the authors of which I forbear to name, which give instructions how to stain crystal in such a way as to imitate emerald and other transparent stones; how to make sardonyx of sarda, and other gems in a similar manner. Indeed, there is no kind of fraud practised by which larger profits are made."

If, as Pliny says, the makers of false stones had become masters in the art of imitation, it yet appears that their productions were not so unrecognizable that an accustomed eye could not discover the fraud. It is recorded that Cornelia Salonia, the wife of the emperor Gallienus, bought from a lapidary a splendid set of stones which he sold as real but which were recognized to be false.

To deceive a sovereign has always been a capital offence, and so Gallienus without any ceremony condemned the merchant to be thrown to the lions; an imperial idea which was all the more happy that it allowed him at once to avenge the insult offered to the crown and to offer a spectacle to the Roman populace. On the day so much desired by all the Romans, excepting of course our merchant, great and small filled the circus. Wild beasts and victim were at their respective posts, and to begin the amusement there was only wanting the emperor, who, contrary to his usual custom in such circumstances, kept them waiting. Impatience was increasing everywhere; cries, even seditious ones for that time, were already being added to the roarings of the lions, for if the spectators demanded the emperor, the lions demanded the merchant. At last, oh thrice happy moment! the emperor appears and gives the order to open the cage of the wild beasts. Scarcely is it opened than there issues from it—a turkey! Yes, reader, a simple turkey, who, unaccustomed doubtless to the honor of such a numerous company, scarcely knows how to behave before his sovereign. At the sight of a fowl replacing a lion, every one asked in a low voice: "By Jupiter, has his majesty lost his senses? or are they laughing at him?"

After having enjoyed the general amazement, and especially the piteous state of the lapidary, whose prostration was such that he could not even distinguish if he had to fight with a lion or a turkey, Gallienus, who, happily for the criminal, was in one of his rare fits of good humor, caused it to be proclaimed by a herald that he considered himself sufficiently avenged on the merchant, for if the latter had deceived him, the emperor had in his turn deceived the lapidary.

A cry of "Long live the Emperor!" greeted these words, but it was a single one, and there is no need to say from whose mouth it issued.

The coloring of glass,* as well as other manufactures, has had its times of fashion and of neglect. Not being able to follow step by step its introduction into other countries, we must confine ourselves to speaking of that where, if it were not first discovered, the monopoly of its manufacture was certainly longest preserved. This is Bohemia, which held it exclusively until 1837.

And indeed, it can hardly be believed that until that year, still so near our own time, the belief was so generally prevalent that Bohemia alone possessed the secret of coloring glass, that it required no less than the scientific authority of M. Dumas and the support of the Société d'Encouragement to overcome this prejudice, by proving that the inertia of the French manufacturers was merely the natural consequence of an unjust prejudice.

In that same year (1837) a meeting for competition was announced, which was the more numerously attended, as each of the competitors, guided rather by national pride than by the hope of gaining the proposed prize, had only one thought—that of making a step forward in the science whose existence even was denied, by uniting their researches to those of their rivals.

The prizes were obtained by MM. de Fontenay and Bontemps.

* The history of painted glass windows will be the subject of a special work. In this we shall only speak of glass and crystal colored in the paste, and of the formation of objects either decorative or useful.

Although the works presented at this meeting proclaimed loudly that France had a right to claim her share of the ancient discovery; although the prejudice was destroyed, yet the first practical attempts were certainly met with formidable difficulties; difficulties, however, which were the natural consequence of the abandonment of that branch of French industrial art: we mean the small quantity of coloring matters which were then at the disposal of glass-makers, and which gave a certain monotony to their productions. As soon as this inconvenience was known, it was not of long duration, for chemistry coming to the aid of the glass-makers, soon gave them such a quantity of metallic oxides producing different colors and shades, that it may now be said that the palette of the glass-maker is as complete as that of the painter.

Far be it from us certainly to wish systematically to praise French industry above that of all other countries, but at the Exhibition of 1867 any one might have been convinced that in this branch, as in all others, if French glass-workers have found rivals, they are still unsurpassed in purity and brilliancy of color as well as in elegance of form.

CHAPTER XVIII.

ON THE COLORING OF ARTIFICIAL PRECIOUS STONES.

The basis of all precious stones is strass, which is colored by dissolving in it, when in a state of fusion, either of certain metallic or other oxides, or of gold, silver, sulphur, charcoal, etc.

Strass, a crystalline substance very rich in lead, was produced about the commencement of the present century by an artist who gave it his name. The following are its constituent parts according to M. Dumas:

```
Silica..................................38·2
Oxide of lead..........................53·0
Potash................................. 7·8
Alumina, borax, arsenic acid..........Traces.
```

We shall now give the formulæ, according to M. Péligot, employed for the fabrication of the artificial precious stones most frequently used, referring the reader to M. Lançon's work* for all the others.

Amethyst.—1000 parts of strass and 25 of oxide of cobalt.

---

* *L'Art du Lapidaire*, Paris, Garnier, 1830.

Aventurine.—The etymology of this word is not known. According to some it owes its name to its resemblance to quartz aventurine, and, according to others, to the happy awkwardness of a workman who dropped by accident some filings into a pot containing glass in a state of fusion. Its manufacture, which is of Venetian origin, is still monopolized by two or three glass-makers who work it alone, and keep the process secret. From this arises the dearness of this stone, the price of which varies from £1 to £3 the pound.

According to M. Péligot, "the aventurine is a yellowish glass, in which there are an infinite number of small crystals of copper, protoxide of copper, or silicate of that oxide. When it is polished, this glass presents, especially in the light, a glittering appearance, which causes its being employed in jewellery.

"Many attempts have been made to discover the secret of its manufacture. A skilful chemist, M. Hautefeuille, has succeeded by persevering efforts in making this glass in considerable quantities: he has just published in the last report of the Société d'Encouragement (October, 1860) a memoir in which he freely indicates the processes he has followed.

"When the glass is very liquid, iron or fine brass turnings enclosed in paper are added; these are incorporated into it by stirring the glass with a red-hot iron rod. The glass becomes blood red, opaque, and at the same time milky and full of bubbles; the draught of the furnace is then stopped, the ash-pan

"The iron rod which is fixed perpendicularly on the table receives a sort of wooden sheath bristling with small iron points serving to hold the stick firmly which is in the workman's right hand, and by means of which the stone is held conveniently on the wheel, which is sometimes of lead, sometimes of tin, copper, or even of wood, and on which is laid emery, tripoli, pumice, or putty, according to the nature and hardness of the stones which are to be cut and polished. When a careful cutting is required for a valuable stone, the lapidaries do not hold the cement sticks in their hands; they use a rather complicated support called *cadran;* it is fixed on the rod and receives the extremity of the little wooden handles. The lapidary is seated on a chair or a stool at the side, opposite, and in the middle of the mill; he turns the handle with his left hand, and with the other he holds his stone on the wheel to cut and polish it."

CHAPTER XIX.

FILIGREE GLASS.

The name of filigree glass is given to those glasses composed of a greater or less number of small rods, either of opaque white glass, called at Venice *latticinio* (milk white), or of glass colored in the mass and covered with a light coating of white glass.

Although general opinion attributes the invention of filigree glass to the glass-makers of Venice, we think it necessary to quote here a sentence of a letter, written from Rome by the Abbé Barthélemy to the Comte de Caylus, the 25th of December, 1756:*
"I am especially pleased with a little ball of a pale yellow color, with clusters of white enamel ranged inside perpendicularly around the circumference."

If, as these words of the learned archæologist sufficiently demonstrate, the priority of the invention of filigree glass belongs to antiquity, it would still be unjust to deny to the Venetians the happy extension they have given to this sort of ornament, which takes an important part in their most prized productions.

---

* The abbé J. J. Barthélémy, born 1716, at Cassis (Provence), died at Paris, 1795, was a learned French archæologist, the author of several works, amongst others of the *Voyage du Jeune Anacharsis*.

The general interest attaching to this kind of manufacture, long surrounded by mystery, and the difficulty felt in understanding by what process the glass-makers of Murano succeeded in preserving, without any change or irregularity, those fine and delicate designs, either white or colored, placed in the centre of a colorless glass, make us hope that the reader will kindly allow us to enlarge a little on this kind of manufacture, so highly prized and now so rare.

Before explaining by what means a vase or any other object may be made of many small isolated tubes, it is indispensable first to establish the difference between a cane or simple rod and a filigree.

By cane, the glass-makers of Murano designated a single thread which, placed in the centre of colorless glass, passed from the base of the vase to the upper part, or from the centre to the circumference; whilst the name of filigree was applied to the canes which, having received a twist, have usually a spiral direction. The same glass-makers named this work *canne ritorte* (twisted canes), or *ritorcimento* (twisting).

SIMPLE FILIGREES.

If we suppose that the workman wishes to place a thread of colored glass inside colorless glass, he begins by plunging his blow-pipe into the pot containing the colored glass; then he rolls what he has taken out on a sheet of iron called the *marver*, in order to make it adhere to his pipe whilst giving it the form of a small shaft of a column.

When sufficiently cool to present a certain resistance, this colored glass, still adhering to the pipe, is plunged into a pot containing the colorless glass. Taken out of the pot and in its turn rolled on the marver, this second glass, forming a transparent covering for the former, becomes so firmly attached to it that together they form a single solid and cylindrical cane measuring two or three inches in length and about the same in diameter.

The greatest excellence in the canes consisting in the tenuity of the thread, it is now necessary to draw out this trunk of glass so that it may gain in length what it loses in circumference. The trunk having been again heated, an assistant fastens a ponty (a rod of solid iron) to the part of the glass opposite the workman's pipe, and walking backwards and in a contrary direction to the man holding the pipe, he succeeds, by gradually increasing the distance, and owing to the ductility of the glass, in obtaining from that trunk of glass, which a short time before was only two or three inches in length, a thread 420 yards long and $\frac{1}{25}$ of an inch in diameter.

If we suppose, what often occurs, that the thread is to have a still smaller diameter, this length, already so great, may be doubled.*

The glass rod being brought to the required tenu-

---

* To see the extreme tenuity to which glass may be brought, we refer our readers to the article on spun glass.

ity, the workman breaks it into several parts, according to the size of the object he wishes to make.

Having thus described the method of making the simple canes, we must proceed to speak of the twisted filigrees, the manufacture of which naturally offers many more difficulties than that of a simple straight thread. The designs being quite arbitrary, and consequently capable of being varied *ad infinitum*, we shall only speak of the principal types.

M. Bontemps, formerly director of the crystal manufactory of Choisy-le-Roy, was the first to publish an important work on the processes employed by the glass-makers of Murano in the fabrication of filigree glass. We think it may be acceptable to the reader to give it in the author's own words.*

"To obtain canes with spiral threads, which, on being flattened, produce network with equal meshes, the interior of a cylindrical mould either of metal or of crucible earth is surrounded with canes of colored glass alternating with rods of transparent glass. Then the workman takes at the end of his pipe some transparent glass, with which he forms a massive cylinder able to pass into the mould surrounded by the little rods, and which is heated to a little below red heat. After heating the cylinder also, he puts it into the mould, pushing it down in such a manner as to press against the rods, which thus adhere to the transparent glass; he then lifts up his tube whilst

* 'Exposé des moyens employés pour la fabrication des verres filigranés.'

Fig. 42.—Venetian Vase.

ity, the workman breaks it into several parts, according to the size of the object he wishes to make.

Having thus described the method of making the simple canes, we must proceed to speak of the twisted filigrees, the manufacture of which naturally offers many more difficulties than that of a simple straight thread. The designs being quite arbitrary, and consequently capable of being varied *ad infinitum*, we shall only speak of the principal types.

M. Bontemps, formerly director of the crystal manufactory of Choisy-le-Roy, was the first to publish an important work on the processes employed by the glass-makers of Murano in the fabrication of filigree glass. We think it may be acceptable to the reader to give it in the author's own words.*

"To obtain canes with spiral threads, which, on being flattened, produce network with equal meshes, the interior of a cylindrical mould either of metal or of crucible earth is surrounded with canes of colored glass alternating with rods of transparent glass. Then the workman takes at the end of his pipe some transparent glass, with which he forms a massive cylinder able to pass into the mould surrounded by the little rods, and which is heated to a little below red heat. After heating the cylinder also, he puts it into the mould, pushing it down in such a manner as to press against the rods, which thus adhere to the transparent glass; he then lifts up his tube whilst

* 'Exposé des moyens employés pour la fabrication des verres filigranés.'

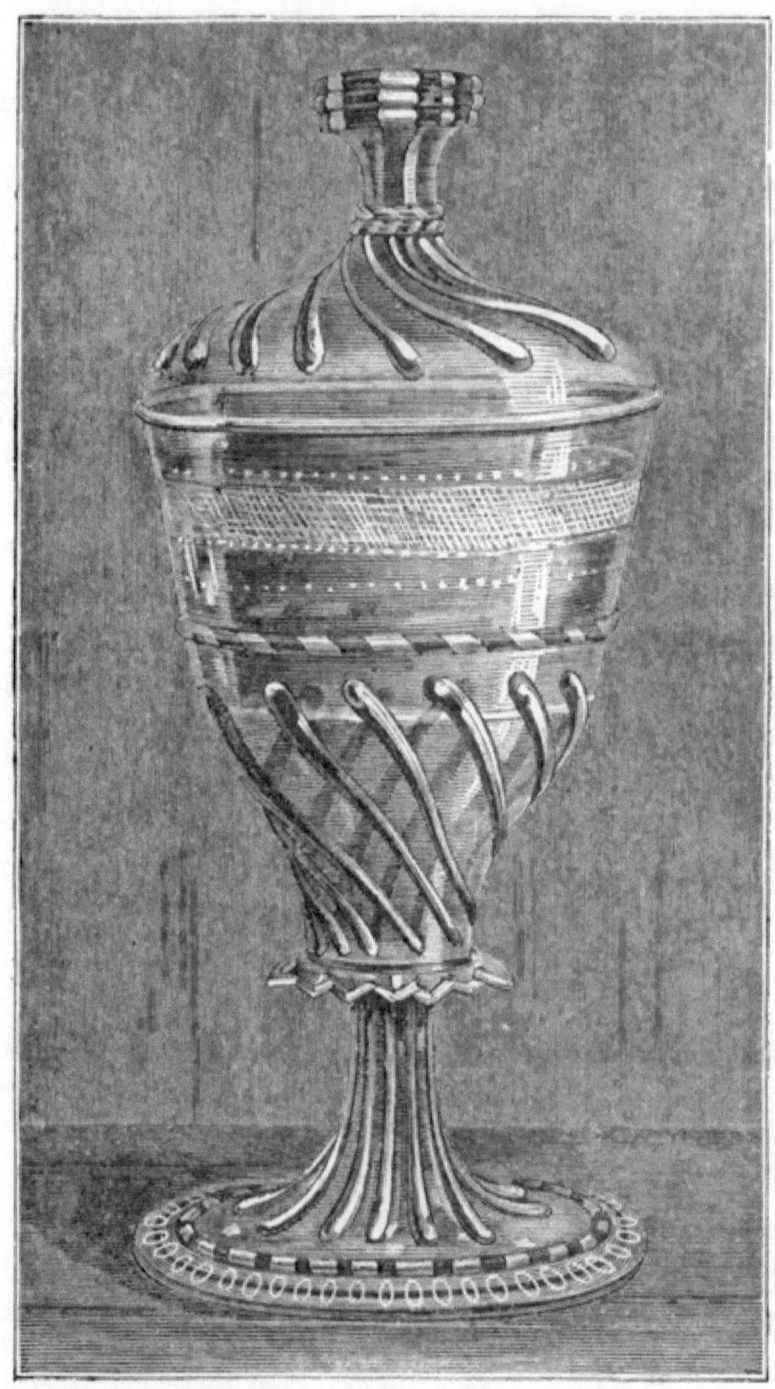

Fig. 42.—Venetian Vase.

retaining the mould in its place, and thus lifts the rods with the cylinder. He heats them again, and marvers, in order to render the adhesion more complete. Finally heating the extremity of the cylinder, he first cuts off that extremity with the shears, heats it again, seizes it with pincers and draws it out with his right hand, while with his left he turns his pipe rapidly over the arms of his chair. Whilst the rod is thus becoming longer, the threads of colored glass wind spirally around it. When the workman has completed a rod of the wished-for dimensions, about a quarter of an inch in diameter, and the lines are sufficiently closely wound, he cuts it off with his pincers, heats anew the extremity of the trunk, and seizing and drawing it out whilst he rolls his pipe rapidly round, he thus proceeds to the production of a new rod, and so on, until the whole column is finished."

The canes represented by Fig. 43 were executed by this process.

"To manufacture canes which, on being flattened, produce network in squares, three or four rods of colored glass of a simple thread, alternated with rods of transparent glass, are placed in a cylindrical mould having both extremities of the same diameter; afterwards the interstices in the interior of the mould are filled up with transparent rods, in order to retain the colored ones in their position, and then the operation goes on as before."

The canes represented by Fig. 43, Nos. 1, 2, were obtained by this process.

"To obtain canes producing, when flattened, chaplet-beads, a globe of glass is blown, the extremity of which opposite the tube is opened so as to produce a little open cylinder. It is flattened so as only to admit canes, and into this sheath there are introduced five or six canes of single colored threads, alternated with transparent ones: the end opposite the tube is heated and closed. Then the workman presses on the flattened cylinder, whilst an assistant draws up the air through the tube so as to take it from the interior and produce a flat solid mass in which the colored canes are inserted. The workman places successively a small mass of hot transparent glass on each side of the flattened cylinder, and marvers it in order to make the mass again cylindrical. He thus obtains a small column, in the interior of which are arranged the colored threads on the same diameter. He afterwards proceeds as for the preceding canes, by heating and drawing out the extremity whilst he rolls the tube rapidly over the arms of his chair.

"By this twisting, the line of colored threads is presented alternately in front and sideways, and produces chaplet grains.

"It may be understood that the canes of colored glass placed in the centre of the column, being, from the twisting, crossed one over the other, seem to present chaplet grains formed of threads having an uncolored space between them, which arises from the canes of uncolored glass alternating with the colored ones."

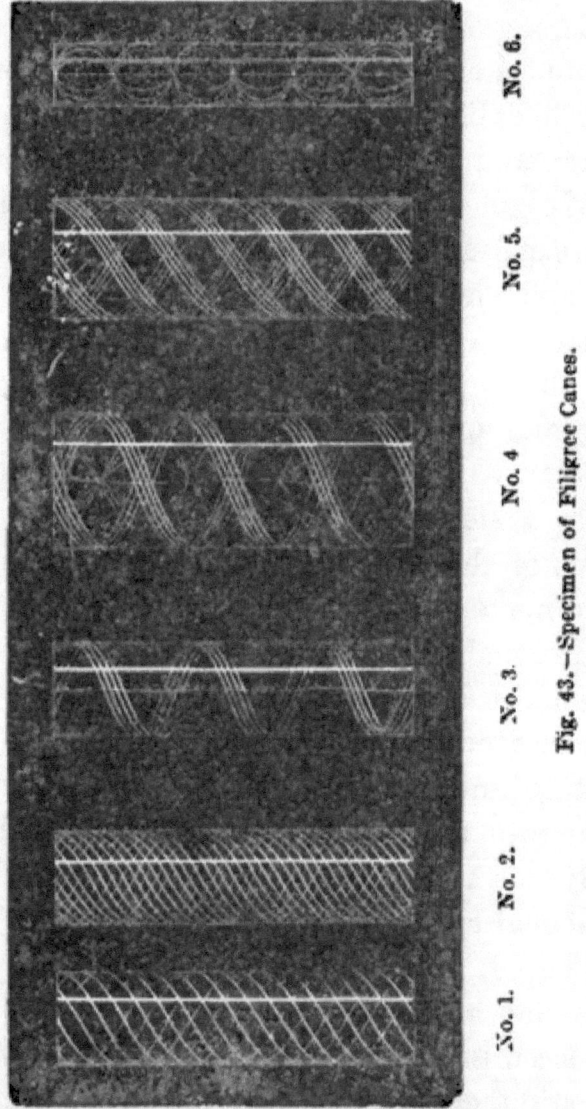

Fig. 43.—Specimen of Filigree Canes.

The cane represented by Fig. 43, No. 6, is the production of this work.

"It often happens that the chaplet grains are combined with the squares in the preceding canes, by using the cylinder prepared for the chaplet grains to insert in the mould prepared for the canes in squares."

The cane represented by Fig. 43, No. 4, was made by this process.

"Sometimes a zigzag line is placed in the centre of a cane. For that a solid cylinder is first prepared of transparent glass, of half the diameter of that to be drawn out, and a small colored cane is fastened to the side of this cylinder; the whole is covered with a fresh layer of transparent glass, in order to produce a cylinder of the necessary dimension to go into the mould of the canes with threads. The small colored column, not being in the centre of the cylinder, will twist spirally round that centre from the movement of drawing and twisting, and will produce a zigzag on being flattened."

The cane represented by Fig. 43, No. 3, is the production of this labor.

Let us now study the means the glass-makers of Murano must have employed in the manufacture of vases of design, colored inside either by simple latticinio or by filigree. And since we have already borrowed so much from others, we will now quote the words of an archæologist whose labors have made him an authority in science, M. J. Labarte, who thus describes this manufacture:—

"When the workman is in possession of canes of

FILIGREE GLASS.

colored filigree and transparent colorless glass, he can proceed thus in the manufacture of vases. He arranges circularly around an interior partition in a cylindrical mould of metal or crucible earth, of whatever height he requires, as many canes as are necessary to form a circle which shall exactly cover this partition. These canes are fixed at the bottom of the mould by means of a little soft earth spread over it. He may choose them of many colors and of many patterns, presenting as many different filigree combinations; he may alternate them or separate them at intervals by canes of transparent colorless glass. The canes being thus arranged, are heated near the glass oven, and when they are susceptible of being touched by hot glass, the workman takes with his blow-pipe a little transparent colorless glass to make a small globe, which he introduces into the empty space left by the circle of canes that cover the partition in the mould; he blows again to cause the canes to adhere to the globe, and takes the whole out of the mould. The assistant workman immediately places a band of glass in a soft state over the colored or filigree canes which have thus become the exterior surface of this cylindrical mass, in order to fix them more firmly on the globe. The whole being thus arranged at the end of the blow-pipe, the workman takes it to the side hole of the oven in order to soften it, to cause all the parts to adhere together, and to give it an elasticity which would make it yield easily to the action of blowing. Then he rolls it on the marver, and when the different canes, united by blowing and fabrication, themselves constitute a cylinder, all the parts of which are compact and homogeneous, he cuts it with a sort of pincers a little above the extremity, so as to unite the canes in a central point. The vitreous mass thus obtained is then treated by the glass-maker by the ordinary processes, and he turns it at will into a ewer, a chalice, a vase, or a goblet, in which each cane, whether colored or with filigree patterns, forms a separate band."

CHAPTER XX.

MILLEFIORI, OR PAPER WEIGHTS.

EVERY one knows these paper weights of solid colorless glass in a hemispherical shape, in the centre of which are bouquets, portraits, and even watches and barometers, etc., etc., but few persons know how or by what means these things are incarcerated in the centre of the glass.

There is a great distinction to be made, not merely between the objects, but also between the materials of which they are composed.

As those representing flowers and bouquets in glass—those from which the name is derived—are the most ancient and the best known, we will begin with them.

The first thing to be done is to sort and arrange a certain quantity of small glass tubes of different colors in the cavities of a thick molten disc, disposing them according to the object to be represented. This done, the tubes are enclosed between two layers of glass: to do this they begin by placing on one side of the disc which contains the tubes a layer of crystal, to which the tubes soon became attached. When this is done the disc is removed and a second layer of crystal is placed on the opposite side.

The object being placed in the centre between these two layers of glass thus soldered together, it becomes necessary to give the ball its hemispherical form, which is done, when the crystal is again heated, by means of a concave spatula of moistened wood. It then only remains to anneal it and to polish it on the wheel.

That a glass ornament, being covered with a layer of hot glass, should receive no injury or change of color, may be easily understood from its extremely refractory nature; but it is not the same with objects in metal, such as watches, barometers, etc., which a far less degree of heat would oxidize or even entirely destroy. The mode of manufacture, therefore, of these latter objects is quite different from that of the first. It is easy to prove this. If we look at a paper weight, provided the interior be of glass, the upper and under part of the recipient will be also of glass. If we now examine a paper weight containing a watch or barometer, under the lower part of the ball will be found a piece of green cloth, the use of which is to keep in place the objects which, instead of only forming one body with the covering of glass which surrounds them, are only placed in a cavity made beforehand in the centre of the half-spherical ball. In a word, to take out the glass ornaments it would be necessary to break the paper weight, whilst to take out the others it would suffice to take off the cloth.

As for the paper weights in which are placed portraits, usually of a yellowish color, these profiles are made of refractory earth, and may thus bear well a heat which only softens glass.

Manufactured successively at Venice, under the name of millefiori, and then in Bohemia, these paper weights have been carried to perfection only by French artists.

The sole difficulty in their manufacture is in avoiding internal air-bubbles, which would the more deform the objects as any defect would be much increased by the thickness of the glass.

CHAPTER XXI.

GLASSES OF CLOCKS AND WATCHES.

WATCH glasses are distinguished as ordinary and concave glasses.

Ordinary glasses.—After having allowed a glass globe (containing the bases potash and lime) previously blown, to cool, the workman cuts with a diamond, guided by a glass which serves as a model, as many segments as the circumference of the globe can furnish. The rounds, when separated from the globe, receive by means of the grindstone the circular bevelling which allows the glass to enter and remain in the bezil. These glasses, as they are usually very bulging, can only be used for thick watches.

Concave glasses.—Obtained by exactly the same process as the preceding, the concave glasses intended for flat watches are made from a globe of much finer glass (glass or crystal containing oxide of lead), and require extra labor to diminish their too great concavity. To attain this result each round of glass is placed on a cylinder, the upper part of which is shaped as a much flattened globe. When exposed to the heat of the reverberatory furnace, they take exactly the form of the mould on which they are placed. When taken from the furnace and cooled, it only remains to polish them with English red and to bevel them by means of the grindstone.

The glasses of clocks are made in exactly the same manner.

CHAPTER XXII.

GROUND GLASS.

GLOBES OF LAMPS.

The custom of using ground glass for lamp globes having become almost universal, we think it as well to explain in a few words by what means this roughening of the glass is obtained.

Into each of the globes, pierced by two orifices, a certain quantity of sand of uniform grain is introduced. The two orifices being filled up, the globes are placed in a drum to which a rotatory movement is given; the rubbing of the sand on the interior surface produces the roughness in a short time.

CHAPTER XXIII.

SOLUBLE GLASS.*

READERS, confess that there are certain moments in life when human carelessness is sufficiently revolting to become a crime.

Which of us has not a hundred times deplored the disastrous as well as rapid effects occasioned by fire? Sometimes it is a theatre that burns and buries part of the spectators, imprisoning them in the midst of the flames; and at another, and this misfortune is, alas! very frequent, it is a young girl who, filled with delight at going to a ball, throws a last look before starting at her mirror; a spark falls on her dress, the flame rises, envelops her, and the poor child, a short time before thinking only of joy and happiness, soon dies in dreadful anguish.

Every one knows of these deplorable events and laments them, and yet no one does what is necessary to render them, if not impossible, at least extremely rare.

* Solubility is the property of a body to dissolve in boiling water or any other liquid.

By what means, it will be said, can you pretend to prevent fires?

If man, alas! does not possess this power, he at all events has that of neutralizing the intensity of the flame, which, excited by the wind, increases disasters a hundredfold; and this means consists in employing the soluble glass invented in 1825, by Dr. Fusch, of Munich, and by him named *water-glass*.

To appreciate the importance of this discovery, and understand by what means soluble glass prevents flame, it is sufficient to recall the fact that to enable all vegetable matters, wood, wearing apparel, paper, etc., to *flame*, the conjunction of two conditions is required; a high temperature and contact with the air that furnishes the oxygen necessary for their transformation into water and carbonic acid. Suppress the contact with the air by means of soluble glass, and these materials will become red hot, will slowly carbonize, but will never burst into flames.

The physical fact established, it only remains to show of what soluble glass consists, and what is the method of its employment prescribed by the German doctor.

Soluble glass is obtained by melting in a refractory crucible a mixture of ten parts of potash, fifteen parts of quartz finely pulverized, and one part of charcoal powder. When it is melted, the glass is cast; it is afterwards pulverized and treated with four or five times its weight of boiling water. A solution is thus obtained which applied to other bodies dries rapidly on contact with the air.

Let skilful workmen take up this idea and perfect it, and above all let the good sense of the public adopt it, and we shall then have one plague the less to fear.

The word perfection which we have just pronounced, naturally implying the idea of a defect, let us see what, according to M. Péligot, is that in the soluble glass.

"A material, even a very fine one such as gauze or muslin, plunged in a weak solution of silicate of potash and dried, loses the property of burning with a flame. The organic matter, covered with a network of fusible mineral substance, blackens and carbonizes as if it were heated in a retort preserved from contact with the air, but it does not flame. It may consequently be understood of what importance such a preservative against fire must be. But without speaking of the carelessness generally felt about preservation from a possible danger, its employment presents several inconveniences. The alkaline reaction of the soluble glass often changes the colors of materials or paintings, and as the substance is always rather deliquescent, the materials, although dried, attract the humidity of the air, remain more or less damp, and obstinately retain the dust. Thus after numerous trials it has been found necessary to give up its employment as a means of preserving from fire the decorations of theatres, hangings, materials for dresses, etc."

After such an authoritative recognition of the

utility of Fusch's discovery, we must express a hope that so distinguished a chemist as M. Péligot may take up the question; and we do not doubt that in spite of all difficulties the perfection called for by the desires of the whole human race may be soon obtained.

CHAPTER XXIV.

FALSE PEARLS.

HISTORICAL.

ALTHOUGH false pearls were manufactured in Egypt at least fifteen centuries before our era, the manufacture seems to have remained stationary there for a long time; for the first Latin author who mentions it is Petronius,* who, in his *Satyricon* (Chap. 67), puts the following words in the mouth of Habennas: "You tormented me to make me buy you those glass trinkets (two earrings). Most assuredly if I had a daughter I should have her ears cut off."

Do these words mean earrings made of false pearls, or merely rings of blown glass?

The text not being sufficiently precise to allow a judgment to be formed, we only give the words of the Latin author for what they are worth, seeking elsewhere the means of fixing in a more precise and logical manner the probable period of the introduction of false pearls at Rome.

* Petronius, a Latin author who died in the year 66 of our era.

If the manufacture of a false article is only carried on while it is the imitation of an object of value, the origin of false pearls at Rome must be carried back to the period when the taste for fine pearls became general; and Pliny indicates this in the most precise manner.

These are his words (Book xxxvii. Chap. 6): "It was this conquest by Pompeius Magnus that first introduced so general a taste for pearls and precious stones."

Before continuing we must be allowed to insert a short parenthesis. Why, it will be asked, do you speak to us of precious stones and a hundred other things perhaps, when the question is only of pearls? To this we reply, that fearing to falsify or at least to alter the text by quoting detached sentences, we give the author's own words, hoping that, if all the objects mentioned do not come absolutely within our subject, we shall gain the advantage of having respected the text, and the reader a pleasure which cannot be enjoyed every day, that of being present at the return of a victorious army into the eternal city.

Acquitted by our natural jury, at least we hope so, let us resume, "sans peur et sans reproche," the text of the Latin historian.

"It was this conquest by Pompeius Magnus that first introduced so general a taste for pearls and precious stones; just as the victories gained by L. Scipio and Cn. Manlius had first turned the public opinion to chased silver, Attalic tissues, and banqueting-couches decorated with bronze; and the conquests of L. Mummius had brought Corinthian bronzes and pictures into notice.

"To prove more fully that this was the case, I will here give the very words of the public registers with reference to the triumphs of Pompeius Magnus. On the occasion of this third triumph, over the pirates and over the kings and nations of Asia and Pontus that have been already enumerated in the seventh book of this work, M. Piso and M. Messala being consuls (in the year of Rome 693), on the day before the calends of October (30th Sept.), the anniversary of his birth, he displayed in public, with its pieces, a chess-board made of two precious stones, three feet in width by two in length (and to leave no doubt that the resources of nature do become exhausted, for no precious stones are to be found at the present day at all approaching such dimensions as these, I will add that there was upon this board a moon of solid gold, thirty pounds in weight); three banqueting-couches ornamented with pearls; vases of gold and precious stones decorating nine buffets; three golden statues of Minerva, Mars, and Apollo; thirty-three tiaras of pearls; a square mountain of gold, with stags upon it, lions, and all kinds of fruit, and surrounded with a vine of gold; as also a cabinet adorned with pearls, with an horologe upon the top.

"There was a likeness also in pearls of Pompeius himself, his noble countenance, with the hair thrown back from the forehead, delighting the eye. Yes, I say, those frank features, so venerated throughout all nations, were here displayed in pearls; the severity of our ancient manners being thus subdued, and the display being more the triumph of luxury than the triumph of conquest."

The anathema launched by Pliny against the excessive luxury of Pompey's portrait, did not prevent the taste for pearls from spreading in Rome, if not amongst the citizens, who were not rich enough to pay for such a fancy, at all events at the court of certain of the emperors. First we see Caligula, who, not contented with wearing shoes decorated with pearls, and having the collars of his horse *Incitatus* adorned with them, also composed for his private use a liquor made of pearls of the greatest price dissolved in vinegar; and afterwards Nero, who decorated with fine pearls his sceptre, his couches, and the masks of actors.*

The silence of ancient authors on false pearls only allowing us to conjecture their use amongst the inferior classes, which in all ages have considered themselves obliged to imitate cheaply the luxury of the higher circles; we must abandon those remote times and come directly to Venice, where we shall find, if not the origin, at least the mention of an industry the first productions of which are lost in the night of time.

The first mention of false pearls is in the year

---

* Pliny, Book xxxvii. Chap. 6.

1318; and according to M. Lazari,* "the manufacturers, called by the name of paternoster-makers and pearl-makers, were established either at Venice or at Murano, and already formed a sufficiently numerous society to be regulated about the commencement of the same year by a special statute."

Although this manufacture already produced immense profits to the Republic by the exportation of its works to the East and to barbarous countries, we cannot but believe that it had not yet attained its greatest height; for the same author adds: "The fabrication of false pearls by the enameller's lamp renders the name of Andrea Vidaore immortal, as to him is owing, in 1528, the perfecting, if not the re-invention of them."

Although these two words, *reinvention*, referring doubtless to ancient manufacture, and *perfecting*, both applied to Vidaore, and the two dates 1318 and 1528, are all that we can discover about the history of the false pearls of Venice, a still greater ignorance prevails as to the mode of their manufacture, for not a single author, as far as we know, says a single word about it.

It is this gap that we shall endeavor to fill up.

MANUFACTURE OF FALSE PEARLS.

The workroom of the pearl-blower is most simple. It is composed of the small table about a yard in

* *Notizia delle opere d'arte e d'antichità della racolta Correr.* Venezia, 1859.

length, on which is placed a lamp with a large wick. This lamp, fed either with oil or lard, gives a long jet of flame blown by a pair of bellows under the table, which are put in motion with the foot.

On this table are placed tubes of hollow glass of two kinds, some of common glass, which serve for the manufacture of common pearls; the others, of a slightly iridescent tint, approaching opal, are only employed for the finer pearls, designated in commerce *oriental pearls.*

The secret of the composition of this latter glass, due to the researches of M. Pierrelot, a chemist who died a few years ago, now belongs to the firm of Valez and Co.

The first material being known, let us now seek to understand by what means from a tube of hollow glass, in every respect like those which children use as pea-shooters, the makers succeed, without using any mould,* in making pearls of all sorts, from the most common to those which in shape and opalescence imitate perfectly the most splendid pearls of the East.

The blower seated at his table has his lamp before him, and at his right hand are placed tubes of about $\frac{1}{3}$ of an inch in diameter and one foot in length. The thickness of the tube to be employed being necessa-

---

* The only exception to this is for the pearls called fluted, which must be done in a mould. As they are now out of fashion we shall say nothing more about their manufacture, which belongs more to the subject of blown and moulded glasses.

rily in proportion to the size of the pearls to be made, the first labor of the blower is to draw out the tube, that is to say, to increase its length by diminishing its thickness.

When the tube is made of the size desired, he breaks it in fragments of from four to six inches; afterwards he takes one of these, and brings one end of it to the lamp. As soon as the glass begins to melt, he blows gently through the tube, which although drawn out has always preserved its internal bore, and the air soon dilating the heated extremity, a ball appears.

It is this ball that is to become a pearl, but it is still only in a rudimentary state. Three operations are necessary to make it a pearl.

1st. The piercing of two holes, for round pearls intended to form a necklace; or of a single one if they are round or pear-shaped, to be set either for necklaces or earrings, or for buttons or pins, etc.

2nd. To give the form, round or pear-shaped.

3rd. The interior coloring.

The double piercing, indispensable for the cord to pass through which unites the pearls and forms a necklace, is done at the moment when the spherical glass adhering to the tube is still ductile. The first hole is made in the lower part of the pearl by the breath only of the workman; and the second is naturally formed by the opening to the tube when the pearl is separated from it by means of a light blow.

This work is required in the preparation of all

beads; but before passing on, we would call the attention of the reader, and especially of ladies, to one kind, we mean *oriental pearls*, which as their name indicates must be the most exact imitation possible of those produced by nature.

Although made in exactly the same manner as the most ordinary beads, these pearls are yet distinguished from them, not only by the employment of opalescent glass, but still more by the care the blower takes in their formation, as well as by the different coloring they receive in the interior.

As for the shape, every one knows how rare it is to find a pearl without defect; and defects not in material but in form, and still more in color.*

The work of the blower being, as we have said, to imitate nature as much as possible, his talent consists not only in destroying the exact regularity obtained by the blowing, but also in producing on the false pearl the defects usually found in natural ones. This work requires much practice, and is only the fruit of long observation. The good blower, the artist, should be sufficiently acquainted with natural pearls to execute on his own only the defects which

---

* A single example will suffice to show how difficult it is to find many pearls almost alike in form and tint. The pearl necklace belonging to the Empress of the French is only composed of thirty-three pearls, and in order to complete this limited number, it is scarcely possible to believe, that after having chosen from amongst all the most perfect ones French merchants could offer, it was necessary to have recourse to those of England!

may increase the value of his work by skilfully prepared reflections. To obtain this important result, the blower, profiting by the moment when the pearl still adheres to the tube, takes a very small iron palette, with which he strikes lightly certain parts of the still malleable pearl; and it is only by this last operation, which places here a protuberance, there a flattening, both almost imperceptible, that he succeeds in producing a pearl which, losing its mathematical regularity, becomes the perfect imitation of nature.

There the work of the blower ceases; for it is then that the pearls which, it should be remarked, are still only objects in colorless glass, are to pass into the hands of workwomen charged to color each of them. But before dismissing the blower, we must be allowed to go a little into statistics. The reader, however, need not be alarmed: we shall be very brief. We merely wish to say that a good workman can make three hundred pearls in a day, and is paid from two shillings to two and sixpence the hundred.

COLORING OF FALSE PEARLS.

STORY OF JACQUIN.

Although the work of coloring of which we are about to speak is the same for all pearls, it will be easily understood that since pearls are divided into ordinary and oriental pearls, it is necessary to have two sets of work-people. This labor is generally entrusted to women; some specially employed in coloring the common, and others the finer pearls.

We shall only occupy ourselves with the work of the latter, which, we repeat, merely differs from that of the other from its greater finish.

Each workwoman has before her a series of small compartments, containing altogether several thousand pearls, arranged so that each of them should present the side having the orifice pierced by the blower.

Before introducing the coloring substance, which would be too easily detached from the glass if it were not by some means more firmly fixed, every pearl has to receive inside a very light coating of a glue which is perfectly colorless, being made from parchment. This layer being equally spread over the interior of every pearl, the workwoman takes advantage of the moment when the glue is still damp, and begins the work of coloring, properly so called.

Before detailing the method of coloring as it is done now, we must take one retrospective step, which will prove that if, following the progressive march of so many other manufactures, the coloring of pearls has undergone a striking improvement, it is to a Frenchman that it is owing.

Reader, I could tell it you in two words, but a descendant of the fortunate inventor, I should say *finder*, having related to me the legend, which he had heard from his father, who had also received it from his father, who, etc., etc., I ask your permission to tell it to you as it was related to me, assuring you beforehand that if it differs from the version usually received, it is merely in certain family particulars which do not affect seriously the historical authenticity of the narration.

Amongst the paternoster-makers and pearl-makers, who as we know formed in the last century one of the numerous trade-corporations established in the good city of Paris, was Maitre Jacquin. An intelligent man, of exemplary probity, and renowned everywhere for the elegance of his necklaces and earrings of false pearls, he had attracted to his shop all the women of fashion in the court and town.

Possessing a gable over the street, a chest filled with good crowns, a most prosperous trade, having an only son who was going to marry demoiselle Ursula, the daughter of his friend and neighbor the apothecary, he had everything to make him happy; and yet Maitre Jacquin was far from happy. It was a strange, inexplicable thing! His melancholy, unlike that of merchants generally, increased in proportion as he became rich; in short, the more he sold, the more full of care did he become. His son even remembered having heard him say these alarming words one day, when he had just sold a complete set of false pearls to dame Roberte de Pincelieu, his son's godmother: "To her also! . . . infamous man that I am! . . . My God! grant at least that this crime be the last!"

Astounded at these sinister words, his son was

seeking a favorable opportunity to obtain a dreadful confession from his father, when suddenly joy and gayety returned to the face of the old man, who giving free course to his delight, constantly repeated as he rubbed his hands: "Ah! France has at last gone to war with Flanders. Long live the king! for, thanks to him, no one I hope will think for a long time of buying necklaces and earrings."

Such an anticommercial speech would certainly have induced the son to believe that Jacquin had gone out of his mind, if the approach of his marriage had left him any other thought than of his coming happiness.

Everything was going on well in the house (selling alone excepted), when an event very slight in appearance was on the point of overthrowing his contemplated happiness.

Profiting by the moment when all the principal relations assembled at his house were signing the marriage contract of his son, Maitre Jacquin, addressing himself to Ursula, said:

"Come here, my darling, and let us talk of something more agreeable, for you have no doubt noticed that in your contract they only speak of death; that is what they call *expectations*. Well, in six days you are to be married at the church of Saint-Nicolas du Chardonnet. As there will be a fine and numerous company, I wish, my darling, that you should appear handsomely dressed, as suits the condition of the two families. Tell me then, my daughter, what gift would please you the most; speak without fear; for, there is nothing I would not grant to the wife of my much-loved son, I give you my word."

"Well, my dear father," replied Ursula, "now that I have the honor of entering your family, there is only one thing I wish for. Give me one of those pretty necklaces that you make so charmingly."

At these words a cold perspiration covered the forehead of the old man which had a short while before been so radiant. He stood as if spell-bound, not being able even to pronounce the *yes* that Ursula was expecting with downcast eyes; and who knows how either would have extricated themselves from this embarrassing position, if by a fortunate chance the relations, who had all signed the contract, had not broken the silence by insisting on an immediate departure on account of the late hour of the night. And indeed eight o'clock had just struck on the clock of St. Nicolas.

Left alone in his house, the poor paternoster-maker passed the night in thinking by what means he might reconcile the promise, made so formally to Ursula, with the moral impossibility he felt of fulfilling it without committing a fresh crime. Scarcely had the day dawned, when Jacquin, who, as may be imagined, had discovered nothing yet, finding himself more tired than a gold-fish which has swum for twelve consecutive hours around its glass bowl without changing its direction, went out, hoping that the change of air would open a new horizon to his imagination. Like all men running after an idea, his first thought being to flee all mundane distractions, he turned towards the banks of the Seine, which he followed by chance.

If the body was awake, the mind, alas! still slept; for having arrived after two hours' walking at the place where the bridge of Asnières now stands and notwithstanding his frequent invocations, addressed alternately to God, to his patron saint, and to his good angel, the poor Jacquin was no further advanced than when he left Paris.

Harassed with fatigue, but still more desperate, he was perhaps thinking of making a resolution of breaking off his son's marriage, if Miss Ursula persisted in demanding the necklace, positively promised by him, when, oh prodigy! there appears suddenly on the water a mass of iridescent matter giving the reflections of the finest eastern pearls—it was what he sought.

If he had known Greek our pearl-maker would assuredly have repeated the famous word *eureka*, pronounced by Archimedes on discovering the theory of the circumscribed cylinder; but as he knew no more of Archimedes than of Greek, he contented himself with calling a fisherman and making him throw his net over a considerable quantity of fishes; for what in his astonishment he had taken for an inert mass, was nothing else than a kind of little fish known under the name of bleak. To receive them from the fisherman, take them home to his laboratory, take off their scales and make them into a paste, were his sole occupations until the evening. The day had scarcely appeared ere Jacquin, who in his delight had not closed his eyes during the night, hastened to descend to his laboratory. Oh misery! This paste, yesterday so brilliant, so silvery, to-day is only a sort of black glue. Certainly any other than our pearl-maker would have gone mad after such a disappointment; but he was a man of sense, and instead of wasting his time in despair he went to the chemist, who advised him to replace the simple water which he had used to triturate the scales by ammonia.

This advice was followed, and three days afterwards Jacquin, who, thanks to science, had at last found the composition he had sought so long, radiant and satisfied, fastened round the neck of Ursula the most beautiful necklace that had ever left his shop.

A few words will explain the just apprehensions of Maître Jacquin and the importance of his discovery, which only dates from the year 1686. It is enough to say that if the use of false pearls now presents no danger, from the coloring matter being perfectly harmless, it was not certainly the case formerly, since their coloring was effected by means of quicksilver, the deleterious emanations of which must have brought grave disorders into the economy of the human frame.

Now that we know the substances employed in the manufacture of false pearls, and also that the interior coloring is obtained by means of a paste made with the scales of bleak, let us take up the subject where we had dropped it, that is to say, at the moment when the parchment glue, still damp, is waiting for the workwomen to add the coloring matter, and let us see in what this fresh work consists, which, as we shall see, requires great skill added to extreme rapidity of execution.

After having again taken up the thin and hollow tube, and soaking it in the bleak paste, the workwoman introduces a certain quantity into each of the pearls by her breath; and would you know how many she must do in a day to enable her to earn the moderate sum of from two and sevenpence to three and fourpence? Forty thousand! For every thousand glued and filled with the paste is only paid at the rate of about one penny.

Colored beads are done in exactly the same way, but instead of the bleak paste, a paste of the color desired is blown into them.

For certain other beads or chaplet grains which are not obtained by blowing, we refer the reader to the article on tubes.

CHAPTER XXV.

ON OPTICAL GLASSES.

The following is the definition given by M. Boutet de Monvel* of optical instruments. "The name of optical instruments is given to the instruments destined to aid our sight, too imperfect to enable us to distinguish clearly all the details of an object which is either very minute, although within the limits of distinct vision; or is at an enormous distance from the eye, although of very considerable dimensions.

"Indeed, in both cases, the apparent diameter of the whole object being very small, the secondary axes passing through two different points of that object form an extremely small angle. The points where the rays strike the retina are then so near each other that they affect the same nerve, and then the sensations are no longer distinct; or else if the points where the rays fall affect different nerves, there is a confusion in the sensations, because the vibration given at a certain point must spread to a certain distance around that point; and then if the points are very near each other there would be superposition of

* *Cours de physique*, page 869, Librairie Hachette.

the two zones affected by the vibration, however narrow they may be supposed to be.

"Optical instruments, by a well understood application of different systems of lenses or mirrors, will remedy this inconvenience by substituting for a direct view of the object, sometimes that of a real and magnified image of that object, received on a screen where the eye may study the details, at the distance of distinct sight, under a much greater visual angle; sometimes that of a virtual image seen at the distance of distinct sight, and with an apparent diameter much greater than that of the object placed at the same distance; sometimes, lastly, the view of a real image of the object."

After such a lucid definition of optical instruments, it only remains for us to solicit the reader's indulgence while we speak of a subject which we should have preferred to see treated by a more learned pen than our own. But if "noblesse oblige," work obliges also, and it is in the name of this obligation that we shall endeavor to show the reader the important part played by glass in almost every science, but especially in optics,* which only exists through its medium.

Although general opinion may be almost unanimous in denying to the ancients the important discovery of optics, we must ask leave to make two quotations which would tend to prove the contrary. The Chinese chronology of P. Gaubil tells us that the

* From the Greek fem. adj. *optiké*.

Emperor Chan, 2283 B.C., had recourse to an optical instrument to observe the planets;* and Sir David Brewster announces that there was found amongst the ruins of Nineveh a crystal lens that had belonged to an optical instrument.†

Supported by these two isolated facts, we may add a consideration at least admissible, if it be not materially convincing. Is it probable that glass-makers so skilful in all the productions of the glass manufacture should not have been led by chance—if their knowledge of optics may not be admitted—to perceive that a biconvex glass, that is to say, one with its centre thicker on each side than at the edges, has the property of magnifying objects?

If they did not know magnifying lenses, we have yet to learn by what factitious force that galaxy of celebrated engravers of fine stones, both Greek and Roman, could, by merely the power of their eyes, obtain an execution so remarkable for finish, that in order to appreciate all their delicacy, we moderns are obliged to use magnifying glasses. We may perhaps be told of those globes filled with water, of which Seneca speaks (II. lxxxiii.), which, when lighted from behind, serve to magnify objects; but, whilst recognizing the services which these globes may render in certain trades, that of shoemakers amongst others, who still employ them, we persist in believing that their magnifying power was neither sufficiently pow-

* *Echo du monde savant*, April 3rd, 1835.
† *Athenæum français*, September 18th, 1852.

erful, nor sufficiently clear, regular, and practical, to be utilized by artists. Although palpable proofs are as yet wanting, it may be only a delay for the cause of the ancients; for the researches undertaken a few years ago have already brought to light so many objects, the knowledge of which was refused to them in past centuries, that there is nothing to indicate that it will not be the same in optical glasses.

Leaving the cause of the ancients, it remains for us to show the immense services that glass has rendered and still renders to humanity, as well as to the sciences, which owe their progress to it; to make known the name and method of manufacture employed in each of them; and lastly, the reason for the employment of one or more glasses in optical instruments. To attain this result, we shall often neglect the external part of the instrument, which every one is acquainted with, and occupy ourselves exclusively with the interior, for it is that alone which can teach us the different use of each kind of glass.

But before going farther, and at the risk of being unintelligible, we must say a word about light,* as well as on its relation to optics.

What was light less than two hundred years ago? A vague, colorless thing, which every one used without troubling themselves in the slightest degree about the different parts which might compose it; when the

---

* Light comes to us from the sun in eight minutes thirteen seconds. To reach us it traverses in this short time 77,000 leagues.

illustrious Newton,* more curious than the generality of men, took it into his head to force light, which had been left very quiet until then, to divulge its secrets to him. He set to work then, and Europe soon learned not only that light was decomposable, but that it was composed of seven colors—red, orange, yellow, green, blue, indigo, and violet.†

But how did he make this astonishing discovery? How many enormous, complicated instruments was he obliged to use? What shape were they? Do they still exist, and can they be seen?

Such, dear readers, are the questions I shall be asked; so I shall tell you at once that they do exist, and that all the apparatus of machinery which your imagination has conjured up was kept in Newton's pocket, for it was a simple little piece of glass, known in optics by the name of prism.

As the prism played the principal, we may even say the only part in the discovery, let us say a word on its form, and pass afterwards to the explanation of a phenomenon which every one can easily repeat at home, so simple and easy is it.

THE PRISM.

In dioptrics ‡ the name of prism is given to a

* Sir Isaac Newton, born at Woolsthorpe (Lincoln), in 1642, died in 1727.

† This phenomenon is termed dispersion.

‡ From the Greek *dia*, through, and *optomai*, to see. In its most extended sense, the object of dioptrics is to consider and explain the effects of the refraction of light when it passes through different mediums, such as air, water, glass, and especially lenses.

transparent solid having the figure of a triangular prism, that is to say, whose two extremities form two equal and parallel triangles, and whose three other faces, which circumscribe the form, are highly pol-

V Violet. *I* Indigo. *B* Blue. *V* Green. *J* Yellow. *O* Orange. *R* Red.
Fig. 45.—Solar Spectrum.

ished parallelograms. For the convenience of the observer, the prism is generally adapted to a metallic stand with a screw, allowing it to be placed at whatever height and inclination are desired.

To obtain this remarkable effect it requires a totally dark room, only receiving light from a small opening made in the shutter, some fractions of an inch in diameter, by which a ray of the sun will pass, called a *pencil of solar light*, S.

Without a prism, this pencil falling directly on the floor, S, will form a round white image; but if a prism of flint glass, P, be placed horizontally before the opening, the scene changes, for the pencil of light on entering and leaving the prism is immediately refracted * towards the base of the latter, and instead of the colorless image which we had just now on the floor, S, we see on a screen about five or six yards distant † an image E, colored with the lovely hues of the rainbow.

This image is called the *solar spectrum*. Seven principal colors, as we have said, may be distinguished in it—red, orange, yellow, green, blue, indigo, and violet.

Light being decomposed into colored rays, it remains to seek the means to reproduce it colorless, such as it was before passing through the prism. If Euler ‡ was the first who resolved the problem, Hall and then Dollond created *achromatism*,§ which, destroying in glasses the superfluous colors in light, only allows those to be seen which are the colors of the objects looked at.

---

* By refraction is meant the deviation experienced by the luminous rays when they pass obliquely from one medium to another.

† The refracting angle of the prism being of sixty degrees, the screen on which the spectrum is received should be from five to six yards distant. Ganot, *Physique*, page 418.

‡ Leonard Euler, a celebrated geometrician, born at Basle, 1707. Although he became blind when fifty-nine, he continued to devote himself to study. He died in 1783.

§ From *a*, without, and *chroma*, color.

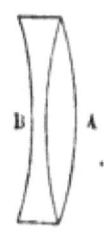

Fig. 46.

Achromatism is obtained by combining, according to certain rules, two sorts of glasses, one of crown glass the other of flint glass, united or glued together.*

There are several means of decomposing the solar spectrum and restoring the white color to light. We will confine ourselves to describing three.

The first consists in causing the solar spectrum to pass through another prism of the same refracting angle as the first, but turned in an opposite direction.

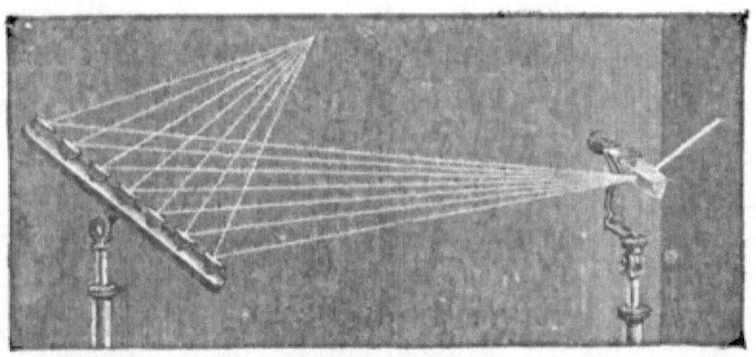

Fig. 47.—Recomposition of Light.

The second is by receiving the spectral line on a biconvex lens, behind which is placed a small screen of pasteboard, which receives all the rays as white.

The third method consists in receiving on seven small glass mirrors, with their faces quite parallel, the seven colors of the spectrum (Fig. 47).

* These glasses are gummed together when hot by means of a transparent resin, called Canada balsam, a sort of turpentine of perfect liquidity.

ON OPTICAL GLASSES.

The mirrors being suitably directed, the seven reflected pencils are first made to fall on the ceiling, so as to form there seven distinct images, violet, indigo, blue, green, yellow, orange, and red. Then moving the mirrors in such a manner that the seven images come exactly over each other, a single image is thus obtained, which is white.

COMPOSITION OF OPTICAL GLASS.

The glasses intended for optics, having necessarily not only an exceptional transparence and limpidity, but being also obliged to be of two different densities in order to become achromatic, are, as we have just said, *flint glass* (ordinary crystal containing lead), and *crown glass* (sheet glass which in the process of making takes the form of a crown).

FLINT GLASS.

According to M. Bontemps, the composition of flint glass is—

Sand	100
Minium (oxide of lead)	100
Potash	30

Although the casting of flint glass bears much analogy to that of other glass, since it is made in pots heated in the furnace, yet it requires such extra care, so delicate, and difficult even to describe well, that instead of giving either a mutilated extract from, or a sort of disguised imitation of the work of M. Péligot, we prefer, for the reader's sake, to transcribe here the words of this learned chemist.

"The materials being chosen as pure as possible, the melting is done in a circular furnace, in the centre of which is the melting-pot covered over.

"The pot having been heated separately in a spe-

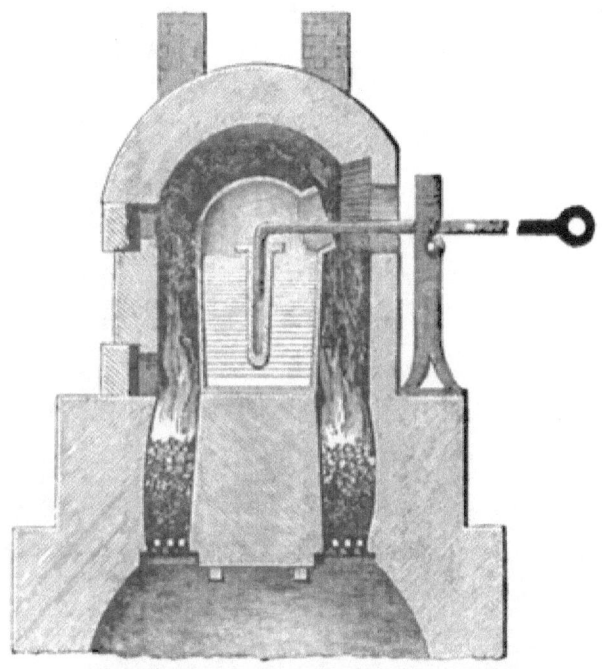

Fig. 48.—Furnace for Optical Glasses.

cial furnace, it is introduced by the usual means into the melting furnace equally heated. This operation cools the oven and the pot; they have to be reheated before putting it into the furnace.

"The opening of the pot, provided with two covers to prevent the smoke from entering, is uncovered, and the mixture is introduced by portions of from forty-five to ninety pounds. After eight or ten hours the whole of the mixture is in the pot. It is heated during four hours, then the covers are taken off, and the earthen cylinder, previously raised to a white heat, is introduced into the pot. A horizontal bar with a hook, resting on an iron roller, is introduced into the cavity arranged in the top of the cylinder, with which the first stirring is done, which serves to vitrify it. At the end of three minutes the bar of iron is brought to a white heat. It is taken out, the edge of the cylinder is placed on the edge of the pot; this cylinder floats, slightly inclined, on the vitreous mass. The covers are again put on and the heating is continued. Five hours afterwards it is again stirred. The stirrings then succeed each other every hour, only lasting the few minutes requisite to bring an iron hook to a white heat.

"After six stirrings the oven is allowed to cool during two hours, to allow the bubbles to rise which have not yet done so; then it is heated to its maximum during five hours. The glass is very liquid, and entirely free from bubbles. It is stirred without cessation during two hours; immediately that one hooked bar has become white hot it is replaced by another. As care has been taken to stop up the grating below, the matter, when cooling, takes a certain consistency, and when the stirring becomes difficult, the cylinder is taken out of the crucible. It is stopped up as well as the openings of the furnace. After eight days the crucible is taken out; it is then broken and separated with care from the flint glass, which is usually found in a single mass. Parallel polished faces are then made on the sides of this mass in order to examine its interior, and see how it ought to be attacked. It is then sawn in parallel sheets, according to the defects it may present.

" As for the fragments, they are made into disks by heating them to the temperature necessary to mould them."

CROWN GLASS.

According to M. Bontemps, a pot full of crown glass requires—

Sand	264 lbs.
Potash	77 "
Salt of soda	44 "
Chalk	33 "
White arsenic	2½ "

Although, as we see, the chemical composition of crown glass bears much resemblance to that of window and mirror glass, its manufacture is quite different; for it may be remembered that glass for windows or mirrors is made from glass cylinders, which, cut down lengthways, are flattened by being spread on a table, whilst crown glass is made without any flattening process, but by the mere movement of rotation that is given it.

M. P. Debette* thus describes this method of

* *Dictionnaire des arts et manufactures*, article *verre*.

manufacture: "The workman takes a small quantity of glass at the end of his pipe, which he maintains in its place by continually turning his tube until the mass begins to congeal; he then takes a fresh supply of glass, and so on, until the end of the pipe is sufficiently laden. As soon as he has the proper amount of glass, he reheats it by introducing it into the oven by the embrasure over the glass pot; then he blows this mass and forms it by degrees into a large globe; he reheats this globe, resting his tube on an iron sup-

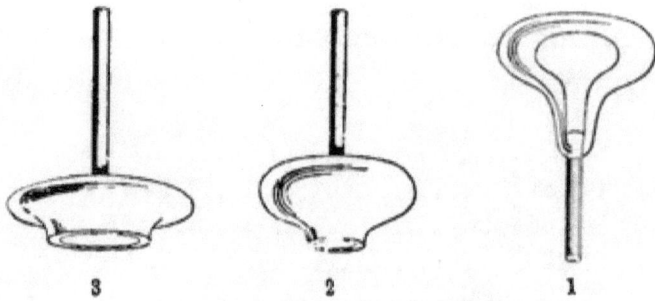

Fig. 49.—Manufacture of Crown Glass.

port, and gives it a continual rotatory movement to prevent the piece of glass from bending and falling down on either side.

"He afterwards flattens the side opposite the end of the pipe (Fig. 49, No. 1), attaches a ponty to it, and cuts the neck of the spheroid near the end of the pipe (No. 2). The opening of this neck is then enlarged by means of a flat instrument which an assistant introduces into the orifice and rests against the sides, whilst the workman turns round the whole and produces a truncated cone like a melon glass. He afterwards heats it again, and then placing the tube horizontally on an iron bar, he gives it a very rapid rotatory movement. By the centrifugal force the bell increases in size, and becomes so flat as to resemble a round table, being of almost uniform thickness except at the centre. When the operation is finished the workman carries the sheet of glass, still turning it, to a flat space in the midst of hot ashes, places it there horizontally, and by a slight blow detaches it from his pipe. An assistant lifts it again with a fork, and places it in the annealing oven in a vertical position.

"The glass thus prepared has in its centre a nut, called the bull's eye, producing a disagreeable effect. If this nut is cut out, panes of very small dimensions only can be obtained, *but possessing a perfect brilliancy that cannot be found to the same degree in the glass made by the new process.*"

SHAPES OF OPTICAL GLASSES.

The glasses employed in optics are divided into three classes:

The *plane* lens, which allows objects to be seen in their real form and dimensions.

The *convex* lens (with a bulging surface), which magnifies them.

The *concave* lens (with a hollowed surface), which diminishes them.

By combining spherical surfaces with each other,

or with flat surfaces, six species of lenses* may be formed, three of which are convergent† and three divergent. The convex lenses give a great spherical aberration and refract light in the manner of prisms, but this inconvenience may be remedied by combining two sorts of glass, crown and flint glass.

It is by means of this union that it has been found possible to manufacture those achromatic glasses which alone, as it has been said, show the images in their true tints, without any mixture of foreign colors.

The forms and use of two dissimilar glasses being known, let us show by what means optical glasses are obtained, which, whether they come from a thick disk or from a simple glass plate, can only become optical lenses by means of a curvature, which is obtained by wearing the glass away with moistened emery on moulds or in copper basins.

M. Arthur Chevalier‡ will explain this manufacture to us.

"The basin serves to make bulged or convex glasses; and the ball, hollow or concave ones.

"Each tool represents a different radius of curva-

* The name of *lens* has been given to transparent mediums which, owing to the curvature of their surface, have the property of causing the luminous rays which traverse them to *converge* or *diverge*.

† By the word *convergent* is understood the disposition of the rays of luminous bodies which approach one another until they all unite in one point. By *divergent* is understood, on the contrary, two rays which go away from each other.

‡ *Hygiène des yeux*, published 1862. Librairie Hachette.

ture. In order to make the tool, the calibre is first fixed by tracing on a copper plate a curve of a given radius. Afterwards two cylinders, one concave, the other convex, are cut out, which serve to manufacture the basin or the ball.

"The tool provided with a stem having a screw is

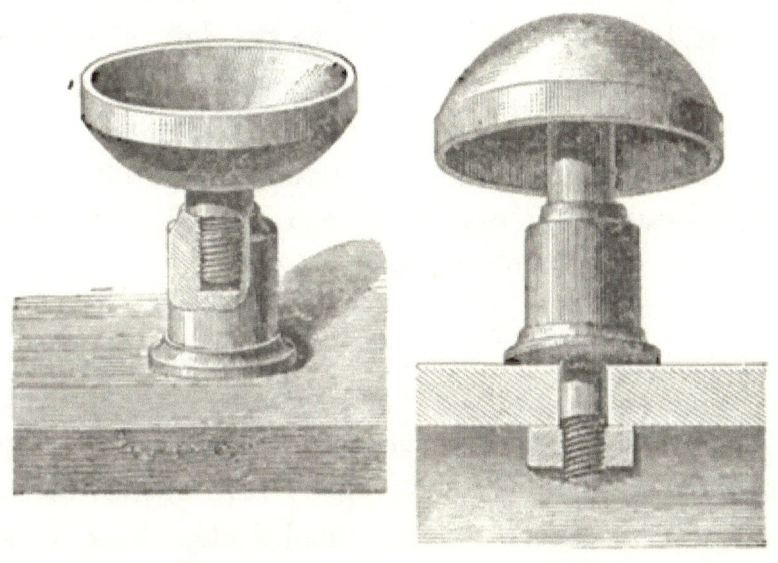

Basin   Ball
Fig. 51

fixed on the lathe of the optician, either in a nut or on a movable arbor, which can move round circularly.

"The fixed tool is used for glasses of a certain diameter. Small glasses are done on the lathe, which is a solid table usually constructed of walnut wood. On the left of the table is a vertical arbor supported by bands and terminated by a point which turns on a pivot in a piece placed *ad hoc*.

"To this arbor is fixed a fly-wheel, and at its upper end a piece of iron, which, placed horizontally, receives a wooden handle.

"On the right of the lathe is an arbor resembling the preceding one, and furnished with a pulley. The fly-wheel and the pulley are united by a leathern strap. The arbor with the pulley receives the tool. By causing the arbor to turn to the left on its pivot a circular motion is necessarily obtained, which turns the tool. If the hand, sustained by a rest, presents the glass to the surface of the tool, on which a wearing substance (emery) has been placed, the effects produced may be observed."

As our aim is only to give here an idea of the principal method of this manufacture, and not to follow it in its numerous phases, we must refer the reader desirous of studying the question to the excellent work published on the subject by M. A. Chevalier.

We have shown the chemical composition of optical glasses, the different modes of their manufacture and cutting; we shall now endeavor to seek the origin of the principal optical instruments, and to show their scientific importance.*

In order to proceed from the simple to the complex, we shall begin by the instrument which offers the fewest complications, and which, from its general

---

* For the instruments specially relating to phantasmagoria, etc., we refer the reader to the *Merveilles de l'optique*, described by F. Marion. Paris, Hachette.

employment, can scarcely be considered an optical instrument properly so called.

All our readers will easily guess that we mean spectacles.

SPECTACLES.

The origin of spectacles is, alas! involved in obscurity; for in no ancient author speaking of glass and its numerous uses, is there a single word referring to the use of spectacles.

The most ancient document that we can quote relating to spectacles, is dated in the year 1303, and is to be found in the *Grande Chirurgie*, of Gui de Chauliac. After having prescribed the use of certain eye-salves, this author adds: *If that does not suffice, recourse must be had to spectacles.*

The use of spectacles was known then in 1303.

Jerome Savonarola (1490), in a discourse on death, informs us "that, as spectacles fell off, it was necessary to put a small bar or hook to fix them, and prevent them from falling."

This is an indication of the first improvement.

An ancient Latin chronicle, formerly existing at the convent of St. Catherine of Pisa, recorded that, "Brother Alexander of Spina, a good and modest man, possessed the talent of copying every work that he saw or that was described to him. He made spectacles, the manufacture of which the inventor was not willing to teach, and freely made known the processes."

Thanks to Alexander of Spina, then, the employment of spectacles has spread; but who was the inventor? For we see that Spina was only a ski'ful copier. The *Florence Illustrated*, of Leopoldo del Migliore, a celebrated Florentine antiquarian, raises the veil and informs us that the first inventor of spectacles was Signor Salvino Armato, which is confirmed by the inscription on his tomb.

QUI GIACE
SALVINO D'ARMATO DEGLI ARMATI
DI FIRENZE
INVENTOR DEGLI OCCHIALI
DIO GLI PERDONIE A PECCATA
ANNO DMCCCXVII.

(Here lies Salvino Armato d'Armati of Florence, inventor of spectacles. May God pardon his sins. The year 1317.)

If the reader wishes to study more thoroughly the different changes and successive improvements in spectacles, he may consult with advantage the work of M. Arthur Chevalier.

THE MAGNIFYING GLASS.

If we are to believe certain authors, the inventor of the magnifying glass as we know it, and which is nothing else than a simple biconvex lens, did not live at a more remote period than the fourteenth century;* and it was to its magnifying power, which is

---

* See at page 259, what we have said about a lens found amongst the ruins of Nineveh.

fifty times its diameter, that Leuvenhoeck, Swammerdam, and Lyonnet owed their success in their celebrated anatomical labors.

The magnifying glass always presents two great inconveniences, especially for scientific purposes, whether it is placed in the cavity of the eye or held in the hand; namely, the coloring of the outlines of objects seen at a certain distance, and a continual oscillation, due as much to the nervous movement of the eye as to that of the hand.

Desiring to obviate these two defects, science invented an instrument which not only destroyed at once the spherical aberration and the movement of oscillation, but also gave a very considerably increased magnifying power.

This instrument is known as the microscope.*

Before entering on this subject, we would call the attention of the reader to the importance of microscopes, which, as we shall see, offer the greatest and most wonderful results, not only to science but also to manufacture.

Holding it a point of honor to bring forward nothing but positive facts, it is necessary to say beforehand that the examples quoted by us, however extraordinary they may appear, have been faithfully taken from the gravest documents, collected by the researches of scientific men.

Four sorts of microscopes are known:

---

* From the Greek *mikros*, small, and *skopeo*, I look.

The simple microscope;
The compound microscope;
The solar microscope;
The photo-electric microscope;

SIMPLE MICROSCOPE.

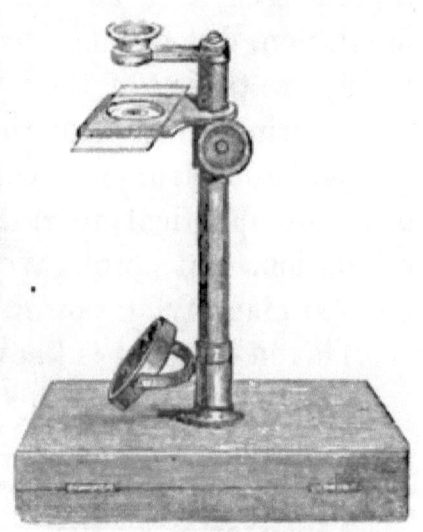

Fig. 52.—Simple Microscope.

The simple microscope is composed of one or several convergent lenses placed over each other, which, acting like a single one, give a real image of the object straight and magnified.

This lens, which is placed in the lower part of the eye-piece, has below it the stage for the object, which contains, either between two glasses or on a single one, the object to be observed. Beneath it, and in order that the object may be better lighted, a small concave and movable mirror is adapted, which reflects, whilst it increases, the light on the object.

A simple microscope may magnify the object clearly to a hundred and twenty times its diameter.*

---

* Ganot, *Traité élémentaire de physique*, page 429, no. 463.

THE COMPOUND MICROSCOPE.

If it is not known who was the inventor of the simple microscope, which is yet a very simple invention, as we have already seen, since it was only necessary to place a magnifying glass in a fixed stand—it is not the same with the compound microscope. Two inventors, both Dutch, claim the honor of the first idea of it—one of them, Cornelius Drebbel, who conceived the idea in 1572; the other, Zachary Jansen, who presented his in 1590 to the archduke of Austria, Charles Albert.

This first essay, we speak of that of Jansen, was not happy; for, notwithstanding the great length of his microscope (it measured two yards in length), the savants could scarcely magnify objects to more than one hundred and fifty to two hundred times their diameter, and then in a diffuse manner.

This attempt, not having fulfilled the object hoped for, remained forgotten until two hundred years later, when John Dollond, an English optician, taking up the idea of Jansen, applied the laws of achromatism which he had just discovered to the microscope, and the result of this was, as we have just said, to correct that aberration of refrangibility which was the principal defect of the instrument of Jansen.

Now that we know the history of the compound microscope, let us see what is its external form, of what it is composed, and what effects it produces.

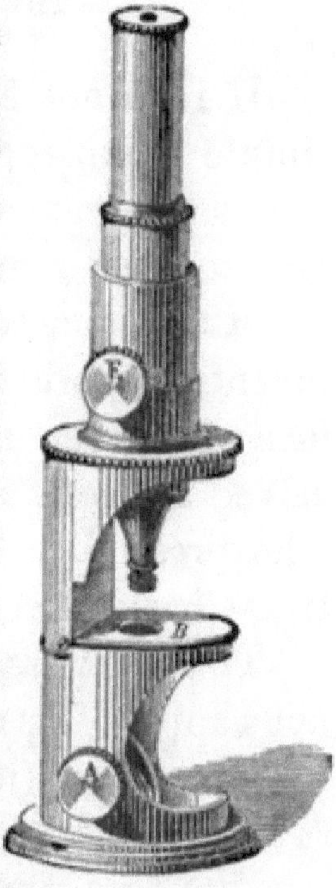

It is unnecessary to say that the compound microscope has the form of a round and perpendicular tube, the upper part of which can be raised or lowered at will, by the help of a screw, E, which by bringing the eye nearer to, or farther from the object, allows the observer to obtain more or less magnifying power. In the lower part is another screw, A, serving to give the desired inclination to the little mirror which, placed under the object stage, is a concave reflector, the reflected rays from which increase the power of the light. At the upper end of the microscope is the eye lens, which, corresponding to the object, much smaller than it, is placed in the small cylinder near the object stage.

Fig. 53.
Compound Microscope.

Under the direction of M. F. Marion,* let us now endeavor to understand the path of luminous rays.

"The object to be observed is placed on a, on a sheet of glass called the object stage. A small convergent lens, b, gives at $c\,d$ a real image, reversed and amplified, of the object placed at a. Another larger convergent lens is placed at B, so that the eye which looks through, instead of seeing the image $c\,d$ simply magnified by the first lens, sees in C D a vir-

* *Bibliothèque des Merveilles*; *l'Optique.* Librairie Hachette.

tual image magnified anew. The lens placed near the object is called the *object glass* ; that placed near the eye the *eye-piece*. The magnifying power depends especially on the object glass. By using three lenses placed one over the other, the magnifying power is much increased. Thanks to the progress made in optics by modern opticians, the magnifying power of the microscope has been carried to one thousand eight hundred times the diameter of an object. It is difficult to conceive such an increase

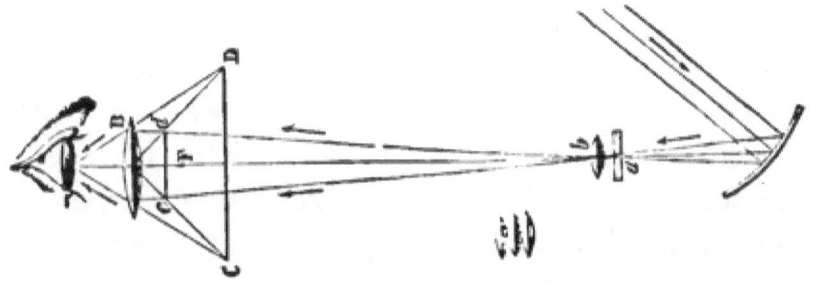

Fig. 54.—Progress of Luminous Rays.

for we must remember that to increase the diameter of an object one thousand eight hundred times, is to increase its surface three million two hundred and sixty thousand times! Consequently, such great enlargements much diminish the distinctness of the outlines and the clearness of the images.

"In the majority of cases, and for analytical studies, a good magnifying power does not exceed six hundred times the diameter, that is to say, three hundred and sixty thousand times the real surface of the object observed."

At these words, three hundred and sixty thousand, which I repeat in writing in order to prove that it is not a typographical error, I already hear some of my readers call out at the exaggeration. There are even some who would go so far as to tax with presumption those scientific men who, in the opinion of these critics, may with impunity place as many figures as they like in a row, certain beforehand, that through the impossibility of verifying their calculations, their word will have to be received.

Do not believe, dear reader, that scientific men, who all descend in a direct line from St. Thomas, and who certainly, even less than their ancestor, can be reproached with credulity, ever advance a fact without being in a position to prove it. This is the case with the subject we are now upon. Knowing that it is materially impossible to prove in the gross the truth of an enlargement of three hundred and sixty thousand times, they have invented an instrument which renders the verification of the results of the microscope extremely easy.

This instrument is termed the micrometer.*

THE MICROMETER.

As may be seen in the accompanying plate, this instrument for attaining accuracy consists of a small sheet of glass on which parallel lines are traced with the diamond, at a distance of from $\frac{1}{250}$ to $\frac{1}{2500}$ of an

* From the Greek *mikros*, small, and *metron*, a measure.

inch from one another. The micrometer is placed before the object glass, so that instead of receiving the rays which emerge from the eyepiece, O, directly in the eye, the observer receives them on a sheet of glass with parallel faces, L, inclined at an angle of 45. Below the micrometer is placed a scale, E, which is divided into twenty-fifths of an inch. It is enough then to count the divisions of the scale, which correspond to a certain number of lines on the image, to know the exact enlargement.

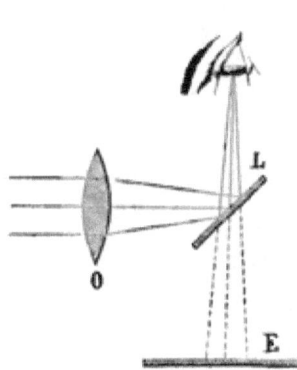

Fig. 55.—Micrometer.

One example will suffice to explain this calculation, which is very easy to make. Let us suppose that the image occupies $1\frac{4}{5}$ inches on the scale, whilst it only covers fifteen lines on the micrometer. Supposing that the intervals on the latter be $\frac{1}{2500}$ of an inch, the absolute size of the object will be $\frac{15}{2500}$; and as the image is $1\frac{4}{5}$ inches, the enlargement will be the quotient of $1\frac{4}{5}$ by $\frac{15}{2500}$, or 300. The enlargement being known, it is easy to deduce from it the absolute size of the objects placed before the object glass. Indeed, the enlargement being the quotient of the size of the image by the size of the object, it follows that, to have the size of the latter, we have only to divide the size of the image by the enlargement.

Now that, owing to the mathematical precision of the micrometer, the most extraordinary results of the microscope cannot be disputed, we must be allowed, by borrowing the elegant pen of M. L. Figuier,* to give the reader some idea of the numerous marvels for the knowledge of which we are indebted to the microscope.

"Applied to a multitude of natural objects, the microscope charms our eyes, astonishes our minds, and delights our imagination, before the marvellous constructions which it reveals to us in organic bodies. A small fragment of the grass of our meadows, the most imperceptible eye of an insect, submitted to the action of this admirable instrument, reveals to us a whole new world filled with activity and life. A drop of water taken from a stream filled with decaying vegetable substance or organic matter in a state of decomposition, teems, when looked at through the microscope, with myriads of living beings, with creatures having each a separate organisation, and accomplishing their physiological functions like the larger animals which are known to us.

"The revelation of this invisible world, which the ancients did not know,† is an additional motive for us moderns to admire the omnipotence of the Creator.

* *Les Grandes Inventions Anciennes et Modernes*, page 155. Paris, Hachette, 1861.

† Notwithstanding the authority of M. Louis Figuier, we must still express the doubt we feel as to the ignorance of the ancients. See page 259.

"In the sciences properly so called, the applications of the microscope are numerous. Chemists employ this instrument to discover the crystals which render certain liquids opaline or nacreous, to study their forms, and distinguish them from other analogous substances. In the hands of the physician it may serve to discover certain diseases by the mere inspection of the vital liquids, the blood, the milk, the urine, the mucus, the saliva, etc. It also serves to make evident the numerous falsifications to which thread, silk, wool, etc., are exposed, as well as alimentary matters, such as starch and flour. It also serves to measure the smallest bodies. In this manner it has been discovered that the globules of blood are only $\frac{1}{3800}$ of an inch in diameter.*

"It will doubtless much surprise our readers, and inspire them with great admiration for science, when we inform them that by certain mechanical means a thousand lines of division have been made in the small space contained in the twenty-fifth of an inch. When we look through the microscope at this minute

---

* In confirmation of M. Figuier's words, we think it will be interesting to give a quotation here from Dr. Francis Roussin, professor of chemistry at the time of the case of Philippe (from the newspaper *La Liberté*, June 28th, 1866): "Blood is composed of solid particles and of water. The water disappears, but there remain concave globules of a fixed diameter. Observation through a microscope makes apparent white globules, which are less resistant than the red; besides, in the stain of blood there are regular fibrines. It is by these three characteristics that the chemist recognizes the presence of blood in stuffs or other objects."

scale, thus divided into a thousand equal parts, each of the divisions may be clearly seen." *

To add to these different phenomena described by M. L. Figuier, and to conclude the marvels of the microscope, we cannot do better than mention a rather new discovery which is inserted in a memoir read at the *Académie des Sciences* (1866), by M. Athanase Dupré.

Would you know, dear reader, how many molecules there may be in a drop of water? M. Dupré has proved that a cube of water, visible only with a powerful microscope, contains more than a hundred and twenty-five thousand millions of molecules. The consequence of this enormous figure is, that in a cube of $\frac{1}{25}$ of an inch, there would be found more than a hundred and twenty-five quintillions.

Let us thank M. Dupré for having kindly omitted the fractions.

Before concluding the wonders of the microscope, which wonders, however, we might easily multiply, there is one thing to which we would invite the reader's special attention, because, as it destroys the only defect of the microscope, it has become its almost indispensable accompaniment.

Indeed, although the microscope has the power of magnifying objects to such a degree that it opens to our observation a whole world which the visual organs would not perceive without its aid, it must be recognized that the enlargement obtained escapes us

* See page 282, what has been said on the micrometer.

as soon as our eye is no longer applied to the eyepiece. From this arises the impossibility of preserving the result, the complete and real figuring of the magnified object, which being only compared with our remembrances, becomes consequently fugitive, doubtful, and always erroneous.

Amongst the intelligent discoveries due to the MM. Nachet, opticians, there is one which enters too much into our subject for us not to mention the revolution it has introduced into microscopic observations.

Alone, as we have just said, the microscope only offers a passing image, incapable of being fixed; ., thanks to the Nachet prism (camera lucida), the alargement given by the microscope, the infinite details of form which it presents to the sight, are placed on paper by the observer's own hand.

We give the reader the few lines that the MM. Nachet have kindly sent us on the effect of their prism adapted to the microscope.

"This apparatus, which may be termed a *camera lucida*, consists of a glass prism, A, B, C, D, of an almost rhomboid shape. To the face A, C, there is applied, by means of a transparent matter, a small prism, E, constructed and placed in such a manner that one of its faces is parallel to the face A, B, so that the rays leaving the eye-piece, O, of the microscope may reach the eye placed at I without undergoing any refraction, just as if one looked through a sheet of glass with parallel surfaces. Now if we

ON OPTICAL GLASSES.

place a pencil, F, under the face B, D, its image reflected by that face will be sent on the face A, C, and reflected it will reach the eye, which at the same time perceives the object seen in the microscope. The two impressions being superimposed in the eye, nothing is easier than to follow the outlines on the paper placed under the projection of the surface B, D, at a distance equal to that of distinct vision. To be able to trace an image which only exists in the eye, it is enough for the pencil to be sufficient-

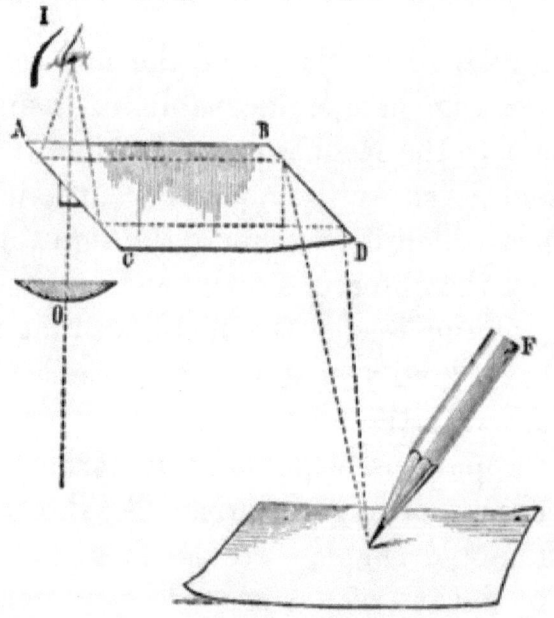

Fig. 56.—Camera Lucida.

ly well lighted and for the point to be clearly perceived by the retina already impressed by the outlines of the objects intended to be represented. Then, without removing the eye from the eye-piece of the microscope, it is only necessary to follow."

After such a clear description of the effects of the prism, we have only to recommend its adoption by all who possess microscopes; for if the enlargement given by microscopes enables us to study and admire in the smallest details the varied and curious forms of infinitely small creatures, let us not forget that it is by means of the prism alone that we can obtain an exact and durable copy.

The marvels of the compound microscope, as well as the means of controlling them, being made known, we have now to speak of the solar microscope, as well as of that denominated the photo-electric microscope; but before doing so, and without leaving our subject, we may be allowed to say a word on that old-fashioned plaything, that delight of the children of former days, which was called the *magic lantern.*

Readers, let not your manly dignity revolt at these words of plaything and magic lantern. Our intention, if you will believe it, is not to oblige you to look at the sun and moon and the usual things described by the showman, but only to demonstrate the influence of the poor, mean, and abandoned plaything, which, perfected in 1675 by the celebrated Jesuit Kircher, is the point of departure, the almost complete type, and even the mother, if we may so say, of the two serious microscopes which remain to be studied.

THE MAGIC LANTERN.

The box of the lantern, constructed of tin, contains in the interior a lamp with a concave reflector of polished metal. Opposite this reflector is a tube composed of two parts, one of which is movable, C, D, and goes into the other. The extremity of the tube is provided with a plano-convex lens or half ball, c, whilst in the other is a biconvex lens, d.

Each glass slide, representing one or several subjects painted in very transparent colors, is inserted into the groove $b\ b$.

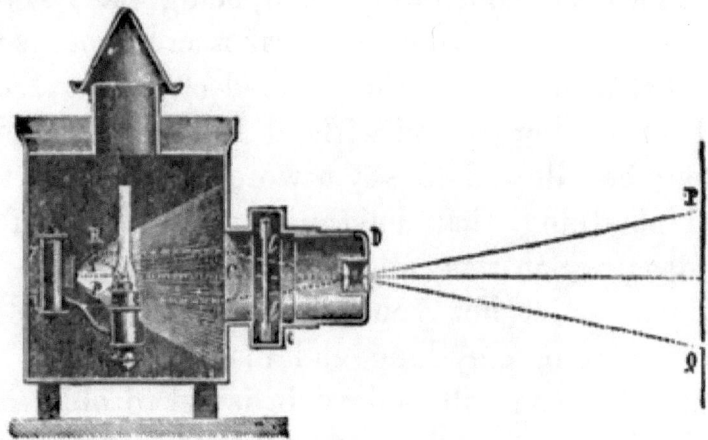

Fig. 57.—Magic Lantern.

It will be understood that, from the rays of the lamp being directly concentrated on the lens c, a very vivid light is thrown on the glass slides, the painted objects on which are thus rendered visible on the white sheet, P, Q, fixed to the wall, and the more so as this is placed in a room in almost total darkness.

The white sheet on which the objects appear being immovable, since, as we have just said, it is spread on the wall, means had to be found to vary the distance and the size of the image: this effect is obtained by inserting the second part of a tube more or less deeply into the first, which is fixed.

As at no period of history, even the most ancient, have men been seen walking on their heads, trees with their roots in the air, or animals trotting on their backs, the exhibitor destroys this unsuitable effect by putting in the slide upside down. Reversed by the laws of optics, the subject will then be seen in a natural position.*

Let us now show the points of resemblance between the magic lantern and the microscope.

THE SOLAR MICROSCOPE.

The solar microscope, invented in 1740, by Lieberkuhn, is, as its name indicates, lighted by the rays of the sun, which replace the lamp of the magic lantern.

Placed like the magic lantern, in a totally dark room, the solar rays are obtained by fitting the microscope into a window provided with a wooden shutter, in which a very small opening has been arranged corresponding to the lens placed in the tube. Outside the window is a mirror, which receives the solar rays and reflects them on to a convergent lens; from that they pass to a second lens, which forms a focus and concentrates them.

The object to be examined is placed between two sheets of glass, united by means of a spring.

* This observation applies to all microscopical labors.

Notwithstanding the phenomena it exhibits, and of which we shall presently say a few words, the solar microscope is attended with several inconveniences. The first of these arises from the constant movement of the light from the sun, which, notwithstanding the inclination given to the mirror

Fig. 58.—Solar Microscope.

by means of a screw, frequently does not permit an operation to be completed. The second is the concentration of such an intense heat on the object that it speedily becomes changed.

This last defect is remedied in part by placing before the object a layer of water saturated with alum; this substance, being a non-conductor of heat, allows the light to pass without the heat.

Having mentioned the defects inherent to the instrument we should be ungrateful if we did not mention some of the wonders it produces. Its power is so great that, with its aid, it has become possible to observe the circulation of the blood in the tails of tadpoles (the larvæ of the frog), as well as in the legs of frogs, the animalculæ—invisible to the naked eye —to be found in vinegar, in paste made of flour, in water, and lastly the crystallization of salts.

PHOTO-ELECTRIC MICROSCOPE.*

The construction and the results of this new microscope being precisely the same as those of the solar microscope, of which we have just spoken, we have only to speak of the manner in which it is lighted.

The lucidity with which the learned M. Ganot † has treated a matter of some difficulty, induces us to employ his own words:

"The photo-electric microscope is merely a solar microscope which is illuminated by electric light instead of by the sun. This light, by its intensity, by the fixity which may be given it, and by the facility with which it may be procured at any hour of the day, is far preferable to the use of the solar light.

"MM. Foucault and Donné first conceived the idea of the photo-electric microscope.

"On a rectangular box of yellow copper is fixed externally a solar microscope, similar in every respect

* From the Greek *phós*, *phôtos*, light.
† *Cours de physique*, page 457.

to that described above. In the interior there are two charcoal rods which do not quite touch, the in-

Fig. 59.—Photo-Electric Microscope.

terval between them corresponding exactly to the axis of the lenses of the microscope. The electricity of a strong pile is brought by a copper wire to the first piece of charcoal; from this it passes to the second, which, in consequence, must at first touch the other; afterwards they are separated a little, the electricity being sufficiently conducted by the vaporized charcoal. Lastly, from the upper charcoal, the electricity rejoins, by a metallic column, the second copper wire, which brings it back to the pile.

"This done, during the passage of the electricity the extremities of the two pieces of charcoal become incandescent, and give out a light of the greatest brilliancy, which illuminates the microscope very strongly. For this there is placed in the interior of the tube a convergent lens, the principal focus of which corresponds to the interval between the two pieces of charcoal. So that the luminous rays which enter the tubes are parallel to their axis, and everything then going on as in an ordinary solar microscope, there is formed on the screen, at a greater or less distance, a highly-magnified image of small objects placed between two sheets of glass at the end of the tube. In the accompanying plate (Fig. 59) the object figured on the screen is the *acarus* of the itch."

ASTRONOMICAL TELESCOPE.

After what we have already said (p. 259), both of the optical glasses found amongst the remains of Nineveh and of the glass with which, according to Chinese chronology, the Emperor Chan (who lived about the year 2283 B.C.) used to observe the stars, must we not conclude that astronomical glasses go back to an indefinite period?

Far be it from us, certainly, to think of establishing the slightest comparison between the glass of his Majesty Chan and those which now leave the workrooms of Lerebours and Secretan; but we always consider it a duty to assign to the ancients the just acknowledgments for what we owe to them, although this was possibly only an improvement on a previous

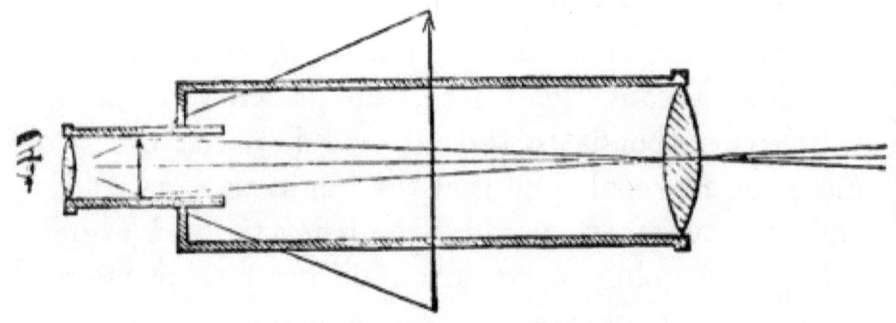

Fig. 60.—Astronomical Telescope.—Interior.

invention, for we must not forget the words of Ecclesiastes: "There is no new thing under the sun. Is there anything whereof it may be said, See, this is new? It hath been already of old time, which was before us."

Now that mention has been made of the ancients, and it being an impossibility to reconstruct, even in thought, the glass of his Chinese Majesty, we shall come immediately to that used at the present day by scientific men, and of which the celebrated German astronomer, Kepler,[*] must be regarded as the inventor.

The astronomical glass, destined specially, as its name indicates, for the observation of the stars, presents the greatest similarity to the microscope: like the microscope, it is only composed of a convergent object glass and eye-lens.

From this similarity in internal arrangement, it results that the astronomical glass presents the same inconvenience as the microscope, which consists in giving a reversed image.

This reversing, which certainly would be an immense defect if it concerned terrestrial things, such as houses, trees, and people, is no disadvantage in astronomical labors, which only observe bodies of a circular form.

Wishing doubtless to prove La Fontaine in the right when he says,

"On a souvent besoin d'un plus petit que soi,"

our glass, so large in itself, and whose power of magnifying is from a thousand to twelve hundred times, is notwithstanding incomplete without the addition of three accessories, which, although small in comparison with its size, yet play, as we shall see, an important part in its application, which they complete.

The first of these is termed a *cross wire*. It is composed of a small metallic plate having the form

---

[*] John Kepler, born at Weil (Wittemberg), in 1571, died at Ratisbon, 1631.

of a wheel hollowed in its centre, and bearing two very fine threads of metal or silk in the shape of a cross.

The cross wire is placed at the exact spot where the reversed image given by the object glass is produced, and the point where the threads cross must be

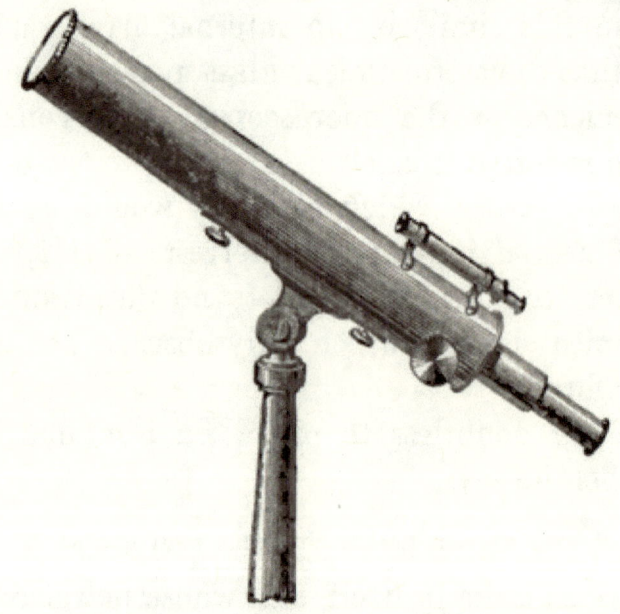

Fig. 61.—Astronomical Telescope.

on the optical axis of the glass, which thus becomes the *line of sight*.

This instrument is employed when the astronomer wishes to measure with precision the distance of stars, their zenith distance, their ascension, or their passage over the meridian.

The second, still more simple, and which is only employed in examining the sun, is composed of a black glass, which, placed in a ring adapted to the eye-piece, dims the rays sufficiently to prevent the too dazzling light from injuring the sight of the observer.

The third is that little glass placed by the side of the greater one, and whose object it is difficult to understand, convinced as we must be, that by its small dimensions it cannot pretend to give the same results as the larger one on which it is fixed. If we may be allowed the comparison, we shall say that this small glass, termed a *finder*, renders the astronomer the same service that the dog renders the sportsman, for it, like the dog, *finds* and *points*.

The immensity of the field open to the eye of the observer in the astronomical glass being the more restricted according to the magnifying power obtained, there naturally results a certain difficulty in finding, in the immensity of the sky, the stars sought for. To obviate this labor and to shorten the search, the *finder* has been invented, which, having a far lower magnifying power, contains consequently a much larger space.

The point sought for being found by means of the *finder*, it is only necessary to bring the star into the direction of the axis of the *finder*, in order that it may be at the same time the field of the glass; and this is the easier as the optical axes of the two glasses are parallel.

THE REFLECTING TELESCOPE.

Although the reflecting telescope,* the invention of which was posterior to that of the refracting, is, like the instrument last described, specially consecrated to the study of the stars, there yet exists such a difference between them in internal construction, that they constitute, so to speak, two different instruments. Indeed, if in the astronomical refracting telescope the objects are magnified by mere refraction through lenses, in the reflecting telescope the same effect is obtained by means of curved metallic mirrors; an invention which, as it is said, must be attributed to the Rev. Father Zeucchi.

There are three kinds of reflecting telescopes:

The telescope of Gregory; †

Of Sir Isaac Newton; ‡

And lastly that of Sir William Herschel.§

Gregory's telescope, invented about 1650, is composed of a long copper tube, one of the extremities of which is closed by a large mirror which is metallic, polished and concave, and has in its centre a circular opening, allowing the rays of light to pass through to the eye-lens. At the other extremity is a second concave mirror, of the same metal.

To Gregory's telescope succeeded that of Newton (1672), which differs from the former in that the great mirror is not pierced, and that the small one on which

---

* From the *tele*, at a distance, *skopeo*, I look.
† Born at New Aberdeen (in Scotland), 1636, died 1675.
‡ Born at Woolsthorpe (Lincoln), 1642, died 1727.
§ Born in Hanover, 1738, died 1822.

it reflects the light is inclined laterally towards an eye-piece placed at the side of the tube of the telescope. It was abandoned for some time because of

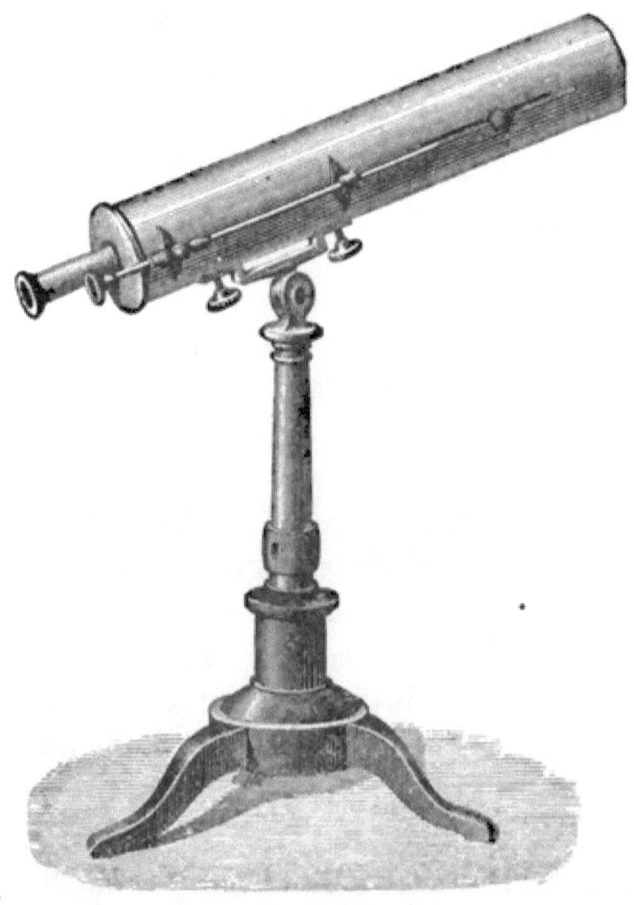

Fig. 62.—Gregorian Telescope.

the difficulty of preparing large metallic surfaces, and only came into favor again when a skilful French physician, M. Foucault, had not only discovered the method of silvering glass mirrors without destroying their polish, but also of substituting a rectangular prism for the small plane mirror.

The few lines that M. Louis Figuier has devoted to Herschel's telescope * are so interesting, that we do not hesitate to quote his words:

"The astronomer Sir William Herschel, who lived at the end of the last century, contributed much, by the gigantic dimensions of the telescopes he constructed, to spread a knowledge of that instrument amongst the people, whose imagination was struck by their size.

"Herschel was neither destined nor prepared by his position to embrace the career of astronomical labors: he was a simple musician. A telescope fell accidentally into his hands. Delighted with the wonders which the heavens offered to his view, thanks to this optical instrument, he was seized with a great enthusiasm for celestial observation. The telescope that he first used was only of a low magnifying power; he endeavored soon to procure one of greater dimensions. But the price of the new instrument was too high for the purse of a simple amateur. Herschel, however, did not lose courage; the instrument that he could not buy he constructed himself. He had thus become a mathematician, workman, and optician. In 1781, he had made more than four hundred reflecting mirrors for telescopes.

"The powerful telescopes of Herschel consisted

* *Les Grandes Inventions Anciennes et Modernes*, page 146. Librairie Hachette.

of a metallic mirror placed at the bottom of a large copper or wooden tube, slightly inclined, so as to throw the highly magnified and very luminous image of a star at the edge of the orifice of the tube, where he examined it by the help of a magnifying glass, that is to say, suppressing the second mirror employed by Gregory, which necessarily implies a loss by that second reflection on the small mirror.

"The greatest telescope used by Herschel was formed with a mirror of more than four feet in diameter. The tube was forty feet in length, and the observer stood at its extremity, with a strong lens in his hand, to look at the image. The magnifying power could be carried to six thousand times the diameter of the object observed. In order to give the telescope the suitable inclination for each observation, Herschel erected an immense apparatus of masts, cords, and pulleys. The whole construction rested on rollers, and it could be moved altogether by the help of a windlass. The observer stood on a platform suspended from the orifice of the tube. Herschel, however, rarely used this immense telescope; there were only a hundred hours in the year during which, under the foggy sky of England, the air was sufficiently clear to employ this instrument successfully.

"In our own days, Lord Rosse has constructed a still more powerful and enormous telescope than that of Herschel. The mirror of Lord Rosse's telescope weighs 8380 lbs., and the tube 14,529 lbs.

"We must say, however, that since the beginning of the present century, the use of the reflecting telescope has been abandoned in France as a means of celestial observation. In the observation of the stars, astronomers now usually employ refracting instruments, that is to say—

THE TERRESTRIAL TELESCOPE.

This glass only differs from the astronomical glass by the addition of two convergent lenses, which, placed between the object glass and the eye-piece, turn the objects round and show them to our eyes as they are in nature.

This addition being the only difference which exists between the two glasses, we shall, in order to avoid useless repetitions, come at once to the history of the terrestrial telescope.

To whom is the discovery of this instrument to be attributed? It is certainly rather difficult to decide, for there are several claimants for the honor. The first in date is Roger Bacon, that English monk who was surnamed the *admirable*, and died about 1294; then the Dutchman, James Metius, who died in 1575; and lastly the Neapolitan, J. B. Porta, who died in 1615.

In this uncertainty, deprived as we are of the smallest evidence proving the right of either of the claimants, we are doubtful which side to take, when six lines of the fable of *Les Voleurs et l'Ane* gives us a fresh choice :—

> "Pour un âne enlevé deux voleurs se battaient:
> L'un voulait le garder, l'autre voulait le vendre,
>   Tandis que coups de poing trottaient,
> Et que nos champions songeaient à se défendre,
>   Arrive un troisième larron,
>   Qui saisit maître Aliboron."

If the reader will kindly mentally replace the odious word *voleur* by *savant*, that of *âne* by *sublime invention*, and we, like La Fontaine, shall also present not a third, but a fourth competitor, who, coming armed with the authority of an old Dutch legend, will once more show us that the reflection of man often takes a less important part than chance in some of the greatest discoveries, and that without chance, to quote again from La Fontaine, " il n'est pas de science."

According to this legend, John Lippershey, a skilful optician of Middelbourg, received a stranger in his shop one day, who ordered two glasses from him, one concave, the other convex.

The day to deliver them having arrived, and Lippershey, full of his art, was lovingly admiring the works of his hands. In this he was certainly right, for he had never perhaps fashioned glasses of a more limpid material or more irreproachable cutting. He looked upon them as masterpieces. So, in his artistic joy, he amused himself with looking at them on every side, sometimes bringing them together, and sometimes separating them from each other. Suddenly he stops. By what miracle has the parish steeple, which a moment ago he could scarcely distinguish, suddenly come close to him? How does it happen that his two children, playing at such a distance that he could scarcely see them just now, he can now see as distinctly as if they were at his side? Are his glasses enchanted? Certainly at that period many would have believed it; but Maitre Lippershey was too practical a man ever to admit that the devil, in spite of his power of transformation, could slip between two glasses. So he began to seek for the reason; and soon, what so many persons would have taken for a supernatural thing, became for him the natural consequence of the position which accidentally he had given to his two glasses.

Immediately he had a tube made, placed the two glasses in it, and the telescope was invented. Desiring, as a good Dutchman who understands business, to insure the exclusive property of his discovery, Lippershey in 1606 addressed to the States-General of Holland the demand for an exclusive privilege for thirty years, which was granted him, on the condition, however, that he should adapt to his glass a second tube, which should allow both eyes to look through it.

Whether this last condition was observed we do not know, but in any case we find in this reserve of the States the indication and perhaps the origin of our binocular glasses.

Three years had scarcely elapsed since the invention, when the telescopes of Lippershey made their appearance in Paris. The proof of this is found in these terms in the journal of L'Estoile (Vol. III. p. 251): "On Thursday, the 30th of April, 1609, having crossed the bridge Marchand, I stopped at an optician's, who was showing to several persons glasses newly invented and used. These glasses are composed of a tube about a foot long. At each end there is a glass, but they are not alike; they are used to see objects clearly whose distance renders them indistinct. This glass is brought to one eye and the other is closed; and looking at the object that you wish to see, it appears to come nearer and you see it distinctly, so as to be able to recognize a person half a league off. I was told that the invention was due to an optician of Middelbourg, in Zealand, and that last year he had made a present of two to the Prince Maurice, with which objects at from three to four leagues' distance might be seen clearly. This prince sent them to the council of the United Provinces, which, as a recompense, gave three hundred crowns to the inventor, on condition that he should not communicate his invention to others."

GALILEO'S GLASS, OR OPERA GLASS.—BINOCULAR GLASSES.

This glass—which was long termed Galileo's glass,* either because it was believed to have been

---

* Galileo Galilei, born at Pisa, 1564, died 1642. The invention of this glass is falsely attributed to him; the real author was Metzu (1609). Galileo merely improved it.

invented by that genius, or perhaps because it was by its aid that he discovered the mountains in the moon, the satellites of Jupiter, and the spots in the sun—owing to its simplicity, bears a very great resemblance to the astronomical glass, as they are both composed of only two lenses. The sole difference between them, which is yet an enormous one, is that the astronomical glass gives, as we have said, a reversed image. Galileo's glass produces it rectified, being composed of a divergent eye-lens formed by a biconvex flint lens be-

Fig. 65.—Opera Glass.

tween two biconcave lenses, thus forming an achromatic system; and of a convergent object glass

Fig. 66.—Binocular Glass.

formed by a biconcave flint lens placed between two biconvex lenses of crown glass, also producing an achromatic system.

As for the binocular opera glasses, we have only one word to say on them. These glasses, now so generally used, are only two of Galileo's glasses fastened together, and raised and lowered at will by a screw placed in the centre of the hollow tube which separates them, and which adheres to the framework on each side at the bottom.

CHAPTER XXVI.

LIGHTHOUSES.

Up to the present time we have been considering glass only as a material intended to furnish objects of daily use for all, and to supply the sciences with the means of studying what nature hides from our eyes. But glass has yet another application, so important that we cannot pass it over in silence. We will now speak of the apparatus which under the general name of lighthouses serves to guide mariners in their course during the night, to point out rocks and shoals, the mouths of rivers, or the entrance to ports.

The services which lighthouses render to navigation could not escape the notice of the ancients; therefore the lighthouse built on the Isle of Pharos (a little island near the port of Alexandria) by Sostratus of Cnidus, in the reign of Ptolemy Philadelphus, 470 years after the foundation of Rome, was not only looked upon for a long time as a wonder, but was named from the city where it had been built. The Romans also were acquainted with the use of lighthouses, for in 1643 there was still to be seen the lighthouse which they had erected at Boulogne to guide the ships across the Channel. These lighthouses, very different from ours, and of a primitive simplicity, were only composed of a wood fire, which, placed on the top of the tower, burnt in the open air.

As we cannot say exactly how long this mode was employed, we will point out, as briefly as possible, the principal improvements which have been introduced.

The first name we have to mention is that of Borda,* who replaced the method employed before his time, and of which we are ignorant, by lamps with reflectors. This first step accomplished, and the career of innovations being opened, other scientific men introduced successively the fruits of their researches, and soon lamps with reflectors were succeeded by those with a double draught of air, invented by Ami Argant, which in their turn were replaced by parabolic mirrors. Having attained this point of perfection, they thought there was nothing more to discover, when Augustin Fresnel † invented the system of lighthouses having *échelon*, or annular lenses. This latter innovation being, with some improvements

---

* Borda, a celebrated French physician and sailor. Made many researches on nautical art. He was born at Dax, in 1733, and died at Paris, 1799.

† A learned French physician and engineer. He was born at Broglie (Eure), in 1788, and died in 1827, just when the Royal Society of London had sent him the Rumford gold medal.

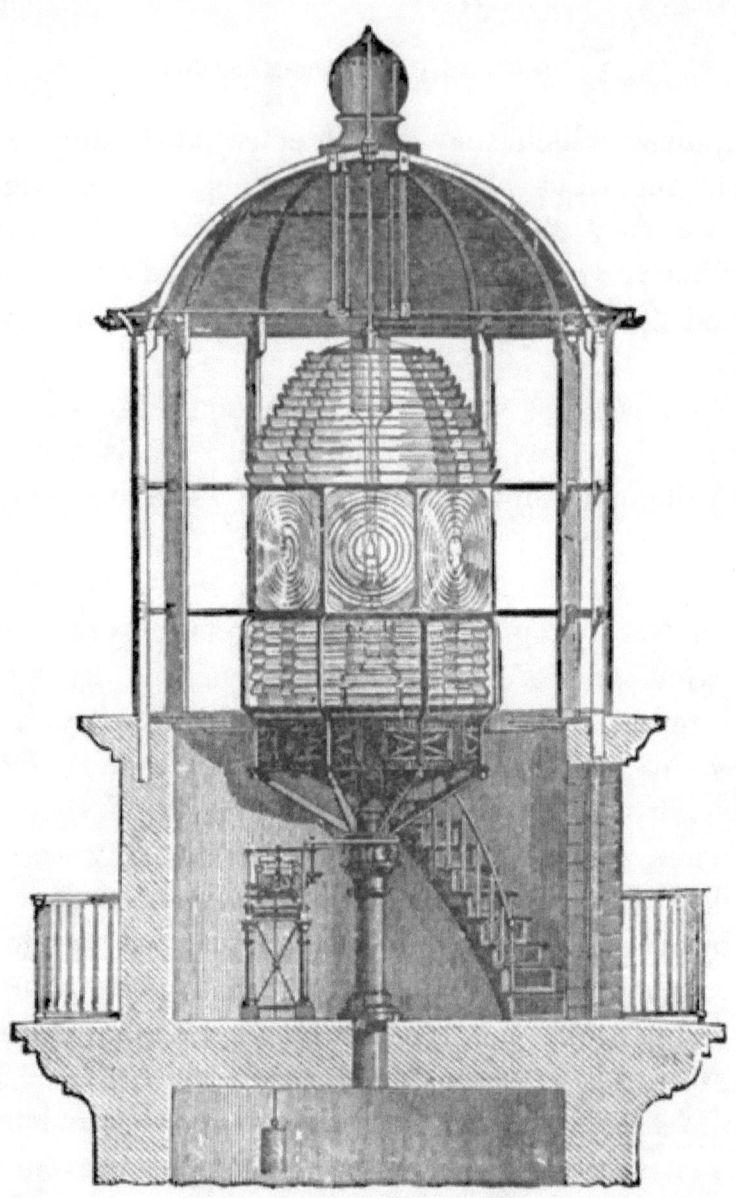

Fig. 67.—Lighthouse Lantern

in detail, the present condition of the science, we will describe the structure, its site, its internal apparatus, and its different classes.

Lighthouses, as every one knows, are concentrated lights placed on a building erected either on the mainland; on an isolated rock surrounded by the sea; on the top of a mountain, like Cape Béarn, near Port Vendres; or on a cliff, like Ailly, Fécamp, and La Hève, on the shores of Normandy.

Each lighthouse is composed of a tower, generally of a cylindrical form. In the interior there is a staircase, the room with the lighting apparatus, the stores containing the provision of oil destined to feed the lantern, as well as water for the use of the keepers, and lastly, the rooms provided for the engineers having the charge of the edifice.

The height of the lighthouses, although always considerable, varies according to the place where they are erected. The highest lighthouse on the French shores is that at Barfleur point, which is 233 feet high; Cordouan lighthouse, 207 feet (almost as high as the towers of Notre Dame in Paris); the lighthouses at Dunkirk, 187 feet; at Calais, 167 feet; and at Beleines (at the western point of the Ile de Ré), 164 feet. We must not forget to mention here the lighthouse which was placed at the entrance of the Champ de Mars during the Universal Exhibition of 1867. This lighthouse, which is 185 feet in height, is destined for the isle of Roches Douvres, situated between the isles of Brehat and Guernsey, and about thirty-one miles from the shores of Brittany. It is furnished with twenty-four lenses, and the intensity of its light is such that it is thrown to a distance of twenty-eight miles. It has been estimated that 2450 Carcel lamps at least would be required to obtain an equal amount of light.

Having described the interior and exterior of the lighthouse, we will ascend to the lantern and examine the apparatus, which multiplies a hundred-fold the light of the lamp placed in its centre. It is known that by placing a luminous point at the principal focus of a lenticular glass, a cylindrical pencil of parallel rays is produced behind the lens, which can be seen at a great distance; but to obtain the results that were desired, many difficulties had to be encountered. First, the almost impossibility of fabricating lenses of sufficiently large dimensions; and afterwards, when this was achieved, not only was their weight enormous, but the thickness of their centre was such that it absorbed the greater part of the light. Then it was that Fresnel invented those annular lenses composed of a central glass of the usual form, surrounded by a series of rings, not very deep, so arranged as to have the same principal focus.

This apparatus for lighting is contained in a lantern having glass of from a quarter to nearly half an inch in thickness; and notwithstanding the resistance they offer, these glasses are often broken by the seabirds, who dash themselves against the light.

Lighthouses are divided into four classes, each of

which is intended for a special object. Those of the first order, usually placed about thirty-four miles from each other, serve to indicate the shores, and to enable ships at sea to correct their reckoning (this nautical word means the calculation of the daily progress of a ship); those of the second and third orders point out the shoals and bays; and lastly, those of the fourth order mark the channels, the mouths of rivers, and the entrance of harbors.

From this multiplicity of lights there would naturally arise a very dangerous confusion, for if one indicated a port another might point out a shoal; so to avoid all confusion a different light has been given to each of the lighthouses. Some have fixed lights, sending out their rays without interruption in every direction; others, and these are the most numerous, have eclipses. Although the duration of the eclipse and of the brilliancy varies according to the distance of the observer, the time which separates one eclipse from the following one being constantly the same, it thus makes known the distinctive character of the light. Others give a fixed light, alternated with periodical bursts of extreme brilliancy, which forms another means of distinction. As here below everything is born, lives, and disappears, to give place to something new, several innovations have been recently proposed to give more power to lighthouses. One adds to the light so many bells, that in case of a fog ships would be preserved from the vicinity of the coast; another still more radical change, proposed by the engineer Mr. Temple Humphrey, suppresses the whole system of lighting, which is replaced by a system of wheels and pistons, which, continually set in movement by the water, whatever may be its level, and driving the air violently through a narrow opening, produce a most piercing whistle, never stopping day or night. According to the inventor, the expense of such an apparatus would be only about one-tenth of the lighthouses, as well in construction and lighting as in keepers.

As we have just pronounced the word keepers, we must be allowed to conclude this article by an anecdote. The scene is at the commencement of the present century, and the theatre represents the English lighthouse placed on the rocks of Smalls. One winter was so stormy, that for four months the two lighthouse keepers remained deprived of all intercourse with the land. It was in vain that ships were sent towards the rocks; the furious sea always prevented them from landing. One of them returned one day bringing strange news; the crew had perceived a man standing motionless in a corner of the exterior gallery. Near him floated a signal of distress But was he living or dead? No one could tell. Every evening eyes were turned anxiously towards the lighthouse, to see if the light would appear, and every evening it was seen regularly; this proved that there was still some one in the lighthouse. But were both keepers alive, and if there were only one, which of the two had survived his comrade? It was known later. One evening a fisherman from Milford, who had succeeded in landing in a moment of calm, brought back both the keepers to Solway, but one of them was a corpse. The survivor had made a coffin for his dead comrade; then after having carried this coffin up to the outer gallery, he had placed it upright, firmly fastened in one corner. Left alone he had done good service, but when he returned to land he was so much changed that his relations and friends could scarcely recognize him. His statement was that his companion had died from disease. He was believed; but from that moment three keepers were always placed in that lighthouse instead of two, a wise precaution, which has been adopted for all lighthouses placed in a similar situation.*

* See the book entitled *Les Phares*, by M. Renard. (Bibliothèque des Merveilles.)

CHAPTER XXVII.

ARTIFICIAL EYES.

In the commencement of this rapid sketch of the history of glass, we endeavored to call the reader's attention to the numerous services rendered by glass, not only to domestic life and to the sciences, of which it is the most powerful auxiliary, but also to humanity, whose infirmities it relieves by restoring existence, so to speak, to the failing organ of sight.

This last blessing has been proved in what we have said on spectacles, but there is another human infirmity much more cruel, for it is, alas! without a remedy. It is of this that we have now to speak.

We have now to speak of the artificial eye, which although it cannot restore life to the one it replaces, has, at least, the advantage of almost concealing its loss from the eyes of others.

If we may believe history, artificial eyes, already known and in use under Ptolemy Philadelphus, king of Egypt, who came to the throne 385 B.C., were divided into two classes.

The *esblephari* * and the *hypoblephari*.†

* From the Greek *es*, on, *blepharon*, eyelid.
† From the Greek *upo*, under, *blepharon*, eyelid.

The esblephari were formed of a circle of iron which, passing round the head, had at one of its extremities a thin sheet of metal, covered with very fine skin, on which was painted an eye with its eyelids and lashes.

The *esblephari* then were nothing else than a kind of small painted bandage, which concealed the cavity of the lost eye.

To this first attempt, still in a very rudimental form, succeeded the *hypoblephari*, which marked an immense step in progress, and already bore some likeness to the method now adopted.

The hypoblephari, which, as their name indicates, were no longer placed in the exterior of the eye, but in the orbital cavity itself, were formed of a metallic shell something like a walnut shell, on which was painted, by the aid, doubtless, of some mordant, the iris, the pupil, and the white of the eye.

A complete revolution had thus been effected; for kept in their place by the eyelids (as is now done), and without any exterior support indicating their presence, the only objection to the hypoblephari was the weight of the metal and the constant fixity of the look.

We know not how long their employment in this form may have lasted, called, as they doubtless were, sometimes by one name and sometimes by another. For notwithstanding all the researches by which he hoped to bind the present to the past, by quoting glass eyes, which have also had their time of glory,

M. Hazard Mirault, in his excellent work on the subject, passes without any transition from antiquity to the year 1818, when he published his researches and labors.

GLASS EYES.

As the comparison of the labors of past times with those carried on in our own days is the only method of appreciating the improvements introduced, we shall indicate the method of manufacture of glass eyes as it is described by M. Bax.*

"The manufacture of glass eyes consists of three operations: casting the glass lenses, grinding and polishing them, and painting them.

"In a flat box of cast iron, without joints and only open on one side, is placed a movable tray of the same metal, on which several pieces of glass forming lenses are laid, which are cut to the thickness and size of the natural eye. When this work is completed, in order to avoid the glass adhering to the tray from the heat, the tray is covered either with a layer of dry white lead or of fine sand. The fire being placed in the box, which replaces the oven, the fusion of each lens begins at its circumference, which in sinking down becomes rounded; and whilst the upper face is thus rounded, the lower one is moulded to the plane surface on which it rests. To this operation succeeds that of polishing, which is performed

* Inserted in the *Manuel du Fabricant de Verre*, by M. Julia de Fontenille. Roret, 1829, page 214.

on the plane surface, and is done by rubbing it on even and wetted sandstone until the lenses, reduced to a segment of a sphere, represent the interior segment of an eye cut perpendicularly at the iris. In order to avoid a partial polishing, which would entail great loss of time, the lenses are collected in a circle, by solidifying them by means of a mixture of pitch and plaster. When the polishing is terminated, it only remains to remove the opacity of the glass, by rubbing it at first on a board sprinkled with porphyrized pumice-stone or of pewter, and lastly on a piece of felt." *

To this manual labor succeeds what may almost be termed the artist's work, for it is to give life, so to speak, to this inert eye by means of color. These are the words of M. Bax on this important work: "I take up with small pincers the lens I wish to paint; I present the convex face to a looking-glass placed before me, consequently the flat side is turned towards me. In the centre of this face I then place a drop of black paint, which I extend until it has attained the dimensions of the pupil that I wish to represent. The looking-glass shows me when I have come to that point. The pupil being dry, I color the iris. The colors employed should be always pounded with fresh linseed oil, as drying the most quickly."

Such was the process announced as new in a work published in 1829. A learned man, however, of

* *Traité Pratique de l'Œil Artificiel.* Paris, Dupǫncet, 1818, in 8vo.

whom we have just spoken, M. Hazard Mirault, had already, in a work published in 1818, traced such just and progressive rules for the manufacture, that except for small modifications in detail, the manufacture of artificial eyes has not made one step forward in the space of half a century.

However, this *statu quo* may be easily understood, from the fact of every manufacturer having as he says a secret, which he conceals, not only from his companions, but from all the world, so much does he fear to find a wolf in sheep's clothing.

Notwithstanding this silence, preserved with so much care, notwithstanding the refusals we have experienced, the veil has been drawn aside, owing to the complaisance of a young manufacturer, the more confiding as his works, from their perfection, fear no rivalry. Thanks to M. Emile Pilon, then,* we can initiate the reader into secrets until now impenetrable. Not only did he kindly show us his casket admitted to the Universal Exhibition, and explain to us the method of manufacture, but he also made several artificial eyes in our presence.

Readers, we are now about to tell you what we heard with our own ears, and describe to you what

---

* As we have considered it a duty to quote the names of the authors from whom we have quoted, we think it is only right to mention those manufacturers who have kindly helped us by their advice. And if merely the name of M. Pilon is found here, although he is not the only maker of artificial eyes, our silence about the others is only the natural consequence of their reserve to us.

we saw with our own eyes. But before entering the workroom of M. Pilon, let us give a definition of what is now meant by artificial eyes.

ARTIFICIAL EYES.

The artificial eye being only a light shell of enamel without any precise form, since it has to be suited to the different size of eyeballs, is placed under the eyelid, and is composed of two parts; the one exterior, which gives the colors of the iris, of the sclerotica, as well as of the blood-vessels of the healthy eye; the other interior, which, fitting into and capping the stump, receives movement from it.

The manufacture of artificial eyes consists in three very distinct operations.* Let us first represent the artist seated at his table. Before him is a lamp, the flame of which, blown by a bellows moved by the foot, gives a pointed jet of the strength he desires, and within reach of his hand are placed rods of enamel of different colors. He begins by taking a hollow tube of colorless crystal, one of the extremities of which, being soon melted by the fire of the lamp, forms a ball when blown. As the color given by the crystal has no resemblance to that of the sclerotica, usually called the white of the eye, his first labor is to color the ball in such a manner that it may be of the same tint as the natural eye.

* It is a remarkable thing that artificial eyes, which require such different sizes, yet always so exact, are made without the help of any sort of mould, and only by the breath and the hand of the artist.

To attain this result, he applies to this ball enamels of different colors, which, amalgamating with that of the crystal in a pasty state, gradually give it the natural tint of the eye, which, as we all know, differs in each individual.

This tint obtained, he makes a circular opening in the centre of the ball, destined to receive the globe of the eye.

When the hole is made the ball is put on one side.

The following is the method followed in the preparation of the globe of the eye. The artist begins by forming the iris, which is done by the use of several amalgamated enamels. The iris finished, he places in its centre a spot of black enamel; this is the pupil, which he encircles with its areola; and he concludes by drawing those infinitely small fibres which are found in the iris.

The globe of the eye being completed, it remains now to place it in the centre of the ball. Nothing is more simple. The hole made in the ball, which becomes the sclerotica, or white part of the eye, having been calculated according to the size of the eye-globe, it is placed in it and soldered by means of the lamp.

That done, and the artist's finishing touch having rectified the small imperfections of the whole work, it only remains to pare this ball in order to obtain a shell, which, softened at the edges, may perfectly resemble the living eye with which it is to be placed not merely in form but also in color.

After having lifted the veil with which the manufacture of artificial eyes has been covered, must we conclude that there is no particular mystery for every manufacturer? To require from them an absolute frankness, while secrecy is permitted to all other trades, would be such an injustice, that we cannot blame the manufacturers of artificial eyes for keeping their little secret also, which consists in the composition of their enamels.

Each of them, persuaded that he alone possesses the best formula producing the most limpid enamels, whose color is most like that of nature, naturally keeps his processes a secret.

We could easily unveil them partially; but besides the fact that such a description would not in the least interest the reader, it is to be considered that similar formulæ are, generally speaking, the result of laborious and often of very costly researches. On this account they become in our opinion private property, and consequently inviolable.

Since we can only speak here of M. Pilon, we will call the reader's attention to a real *tour de force* performed by that artist *without a mould*, and by mere manual dexterity. He produces on a given model an infinite number of eyes, so identical in form, size, and color, that it is impossible to discover the least distinction between the originals and copies.

Such multiplied studies and labors must have their reward. M. Emile Pilon obtained at the Universal Exhibition of 1867 the highest reward adjudged to this art.

www.ingramcontent.com/pod-product-compliance
Lightning Source LLC
Chambersburg PA
CBHW030744230426
43667CB00007B/831